Do It In The Kitchen

Briefs - Tales - Tips - To Set Your Coals On Fire

Leonie Lee

AuthorHouse™
1663 Liberty Drive, Suite 200
Bloomington, IN 47403
www.authorhouse.com
Phone: 1-800-839-8640

First published by AuthorHouse 11/27/2007

ISBN: 978-1-4343-4020-7 (sc)

Library of Congress Control Number: 2007908676

Printed in the United States of America
Bloomington, Indiana

This book is printed on acid-free paper.

Front Cover image drawn by Loren George Lee

authorHOUSE®

Dedication

Here's to my twin sons, Marvin and Loren Lee, for generating double happiness into my life.

Double happiness!

Accolades - Kudos - Thanks

From childhood, a scrapbook of recipes was in the making and innocently referred to as my "gourmet collection." Years rolled by, until my pursuit for anything gourmet resulted in my place of business, legally named The Gourmet Collection Inc. Now with pen to paper, let me break out my treasure chest collection; some garnered from family and friends around the globe and formulated to create Do It In The Kitchen with Briefs – Tales – Tips to Set Your Coals on Fire.

Briefly, let me acknowledge my English professor, who took the time to encourage my love affair with books and spurred me to keep writing. He read several of my essays, but one of his notations remained indelibly etched on my mind. He wrote, "If this is not copied from a book, you are indeed a clever writer, keep on writing." His treasured comments have led me to write unendingly. Confession is good for the soul—my addictions are mounting, from collecting pens to exquisite books. Kudos, Professor!

To my most precious grandparents, Clifford and Cecily Thorpe, words are simply inadequate to pen my gratefulness to the special pair, for being my finishing-school teachers. Papa, he was the authority on healthful living. Mama, a lady with poise, was a stickler for rules of etiquette. One of her pet peeves was that it is rude to rattle the spoon in one's cup; stir gently. Thanks to Aunt Pauline for playing the role of big sister/mother when my mom passed away at an early age; to Uncle Noel for tolerating this "busybody" while concocting his marmalades and preserves. In the process, some of his tolerance and patience fell on me.

My father and step mom, Kenneth and Doris Chinn, made Christmas dinners into unforgettable memories. Their roasted chicken, from a child's view, looked as large as life, like a turkey perhaps. It's crispiness, golden brown color, and taste I have yet to replicate. Thanks to Lily, my elder sister, who always tucked a slice of her scrumptious cake into my lunch pan. To both of my younger sisters, Valerie and Paula, who have specialties of their own; Valerie's Thanksgiving turkey steals the family show annually; Paula May West, her Curried Goat is the "best of the West." I'll hint that I've mastered her craft, but who's telling? I won't if you don't...shush!

To my guardian mother, Mercilyn Rousseau, or Mumsie as she was lovingly called, whose cooking was exquisite, thanks for touching my life. Credits to my mother-in-law, Lily Lee, who never failed to hand over her kitchen duties to me on Sundays, while she caroused with friends, playing cards. She entrusted me in her kitchen, and I gained a wealth of knowledge in Chinese cuisine.

Oh! My beloved twins, my sons, Marvin and Loren, who must have inherited some of Mom's traits - Yeah, that's right! Both are blessed with artistic skills, and Loren has enhanced my book with many of his drawings. They've also had me over to their house for some savory meals. An appetizer of stewed tomatoes gets the taste buds going. Loren's Rack of Lamb, marinated in yogurt was served right off the grill with dirty rice and a cucumber salad. Desserts were decadent servings of Marvin's Crème Brulee and a must-have cup of Baronhall Estate Jamaican Coffee. Wow! Thank you. Now you're feeling the Love!

My gratitude extends to my relatives and friends, too numerous to mention individually. Please know that I know, you are all in my corner, cheering me on! I have gone forward, willing to share my good, bad, or indifferent ideas and eating habits. The best was handed down to me—my best I give to you. Some folks mentioned here have moved on to a better life, leaving behind a burning torch—fire under my tail. I could not sleep until I mustered up the courage to honor them with this book, even at a time when recipe books are plentiful—nuff-nuff, as we say in Jamaican lingo. You played a part in guiding me through my early years—thanks a million! Thanks for the myriad of fantastic ideas and recipes—gladly to be shared. Forever humbled and grateful, let me show you another side of me. Sometimes my slightly risqué briefs, tales, or tips in cooking will pop up, intended to set your coals on fire! To everyone—love, hugs and kisses to no end—unconditionally! Laugh until it hurts—it is the best medicine! Go now and "Do It In The Kitchen."

St. James Villa, the house that Papa built

Foreplay

In this preamble to Do It In The Kitchen, I dare say, foreplay means play with food before sex.

Basic instincts tell us that food and people play together well. Friends and lovers everywhere go shopping or dining out together, and at other times, they choose to eat in. Even if it's a leisurely stroll or a picnic in the park, at playtime, food almost always becomes the opener to foreplay on everyone's agenda. At every romantic encounter, gathering, or carousing with friends, ultimately there are those who find comfort in a glass of wine, some from dancing to reggae music, or "rent a tile" waltz, and surely, without denial, many find pleasure in food and lovemaking—yes, sex! I dare anyone to deny those facts—the naked truth. Don't be bashful, partake of this delectable subject; try my equation, my theorem or formula; food play plus foreplay equal lovemaking, they go hand in hand! It's been said that a picture paints a thousand words, but in my book, a thousand words paint a fairly good picture—the rest is up to your fancy. Do It In The Kitchen.

The kitchen is a loaded territory; gadgets here, there and everywhere—decking the countertop, tucked away in the cupboards, in the pantry, or hanging from the ceiling. There's usually a stove, a microwave oven, a dishwasher, a refrigerator, and umpteen electrical paraphernalia—from a griddle-toaster oven to a food processor-blender. There are woks, pots, pans, bowls, crystal, china, silverware, and a "whistle while you work" teakettle. And, if you're a coffee freak—admittedly, I am one—there will be several coffee percolators; a French press for sure, adorning the counter. Most likely, there's a juice extractor, ready to pulsate some healthy "put it back" concoctions—the list is endless.

Some may handily stock odds and ends, nuts and bolts, locks and keys. Why? A handcuff hidden in the drawer! Am I getting warm or being truthful? Hang a few towels, ribbons, buttons and bows, needle and thread, and how about decorating the wall with a whip for that riding day spanking! Seams do get stretched to the limit—clothes get torn or ripped off, and it could happen in the kitchen. Sometimes the gadget guru ends up with more "gadgets" than meets the eye! One with a brilliant imagination, who allows his senses to take over and uses his gadgets to the best of his ability, will find gratification to whet any appetite.

A kitchen person, I am. Yes, I try everything—once! Then I'm able to decide if I like it enough to do it again. You are about to unfold some of these ideas, some romantic, sexy, sensuous, mad, imaginative, flirtatious, and okay, if you must know, I enjoy everything I see, smell, taste, and feel in the kitchen. And I even hear you—thinking, maybe saying, don't go there! But, that's my modus operandi. My sixth sense "instinct" burns and urges me to take you there, to stretch your limits, awakening all your senses, to bring you to a level of enjoyment with every trick in the book and every meal you concoct. Your juices are flowing and I'm determined to help set your coals on fire. The kitchen, being such a cozy corner where family and friends share happy meals, also sets the scene for romantics of all ages to spend precious moments with their sweetie-pie, lollipop, sugar-plum, honey, or any seductive term of endearment chosen. My task is to pop suggestive ideas into your mind, and you decide how hot you really want it in your kitchen. Things may get too hot to handle—don't panic—if it feels like taking your skin off and running around with just your bones—do it—jump bones if you so desire. Spicy thyme; spice up the kitchen and multiply your pleasure. Leave the cooking for later; be frivolous and allow your wild fire to take over. Dare to shout it out! Eating and romance—never hurt an ounce!

Romanticism stems from the ground but its roots are grounded. Roots represent varied dimensions and ideas; as ground provisions or edible food grown in the earth; roots mean being down-to-earth or getting down to basics. Stretch the imagination further; roots are trees, trees are wood, and bamboo is a tree, from which carvings, platters, and crafts are made into collectibles that decorate many kitchens. Reference is made to the "big wood" or "big bamboo," commonly proclaimed in the Jamaican environs as a man's private parts. Generally speaking, roots and wood have multiple meanings. Therefore, be comfortable using your "big wood" platters or your "big bamboo" cups. Big-up, "big wood" and "big bamboo!" Both are ecstatic and playful connections to our roots.

Romancing the mind—think of the kitchen as an expansive dimension to your life. How about a treat for your significant other each time a splendiferous meal is served. Be inventive, fantasize, try something risqué, create intrigue and excitement in your kitchen. Heat up the love connection with a spur-of-the-moment massage. Make use of the oils in your pantry; blend in a few drops of almond, vanilla, pumpkin essence, or any pheromone of choice to pique your fancy; add some glitz and sparkle to your life. With volts of electricity and fire in your wire—convert the kitchen into an erotic place of pure pleasure for the palate; experience the loving after the loving and enjoy a simple but unforgettable workout. Personally, I never can get enough, so I'll do it one more time, while I encourage everyone to stay healthy—think beautiful thoughts and be happy. Cheers to some good workout sessions! Where? Do It in The Kitchen.

Big Bamboo

Contents

Appeteasers

As the heading implies, some appetizers do tempt the taste buds. Hence, my title "Appeteasers."
Beware, my friends! There's more to come in the categories ahead, especially "Intercourse."
These tasty starters are just a prelude to your dining pleasure:

Bacon Cheese Bites
Cabrit Au Jus de Citron Chevres
Codfish Fritters or Stamp and Go
Crab Cakes
Fire Up Your Nuts
Guacamole or Avocado Dip
Jerk Pork Chunks
Oysters to the Rescue
Pan-curled Oysters
Patties
Pepper Shrimps
Quiche
Salmon Balls
Salt and Pepper Beef Ribs

Bacon Cheese Bites

1   tbsp. canola oil

½   cup onion, chopped finely

½   cup red bell pepper, chopped finely

1   cup bacon bits

2   cups flour, sifted

¼   cup cornmeal

3   tsp. baking powder

¼   tsp. scotch bonnet pepper, minced

5   tbsp. butter, chilled

1   cup cheddar cheese, shredded

1   cup cream or buttermilk

In a sauté pan, heat oil, add onion, and cook until transparent. Add pepper and bacon. Cook for a minute. Remove pan from heat. Preheat oven to 450° F. Grease cookie sheet. In a mixing bowl, add flour, cornmeal, sugar, baking powder, and pepper. Use two knives to cut the butter into the flour, to form a crumb-like mixture. Add bacon mixture and cheese. Open a well in the center. Add the buttermilk and stir with a fork to form dough. With a floured rolling pin, press the dough to about a half-inch thick on a pastry sheet. Cut about 16 two-inch rounds. Set them on the cookie sheet, one inch apart, and bake for 10–12 minutes until done. Serves 8.

☙

To ensure your biscuits are light and fluffy, keep the butter chilled until ready to use; handle the dough as little as possible; cut into the batter quickly and use cold hands for kneading. These are savory bites that disappear in a blink.

Cabrit au Jus de Citron - Chevres

3   lbs. goat meat (leg cut in 2-inch pieces)

2   limes or lemons

3   cloves garlic, diced finely

1   tsp. salt

1   whole scotch bonnet pepper

4   cloves

1   large onion, chopped

2   tbsp. each canola and olive oil

2   stalks escallion (green onion), fresh parsley, or cilantro leaves, chopped.

Clean and wash meat thoroughly with lime or lemon juice. Cover meat with sufficient water to bring to boil. Add garlic, salt, pepper, cloves, and onion. Cook until tender, but not falling off the bone. Remove meat from liquid, and drain. Drizzle with olive and canola oil. Add lemon or lime juice, salt and pepper to taste. Broil, bake, fry or brown on the barbecue grill until tender and crispy. Garnish with parsley, cilantro, or escallion (green onion) flowers. Serves 8.

೮೩

To my dear Haitian friend, Attorney-at-Law Florence Verne, who shared one of her specialties with me—thanks for being of kindred spirit over the years! You got my goat and I got yours! Nuff love!

Codfish Fritters or Stamp and Go

1   lb. salted codfish

2-3 cups flour

½   tsp. baking powder, optional

4   stalks escallion (green onion), chopped

2   cloves garlic, finely diced

1   yellow scotch bonnet pepper, diced (discard seeds)

1   tsp. thyme leaves

2   cups cold water

3-4 tbsp. canola oil

Soak codfish in water for a few hours to reduce the salt. Remove and discard any skin or bones. Tear or shred the fish into small pieces. In a large bowl, combine fish with flour, baking powder, escallion (green onion), garlic, hot pepper, and thyme. Mix with an ample amount of cold water, stirring to remove any flour lumps, forming a very light batter. In a shallow skillet, heat oil, drop batter by tablespoonful, and fry until crispy, golden brown on both sides. Drain on paper towels to absorb excess fat. Serve while still hot or warm enough to hold between the fingers. Serves 12.

෬

Codfish fritters or "stamp and go" may be eaten alone or with fried dumplings, known as Johnny cakes. While going to elementary school, there were ladies parked by the wayside selling "stamp and go." Adults as well as kids would buy the fritters, stamp it between dumplings, and be on the run. Maybe that's one of the many reasons for the name "stamp and go," just as there are stories about "Johnny cakes."

Crab Cakes

2   cups bread crumbs

1   tbsp. seasoning salt

4   tbsp. olive oil

2   cups crabmeat, lump, picked

1   cup mayonnaise

1   cup onions, chives, celery, and red peppers, chopped

1   tbsp. each capers, parsley, and lemon zest, chopped

1   tbsp. Baronhall Farms Jamaican Jerk sauce

¼   tsp. cayenne pepper

¼   tsp. grated nutmeg

1   large egg, lightly beaten

3   tbsp. unsalted butter

In a bowl, mix bread crumbs, seasoning salt, and half the olive oil, and set aside. In another bowl, combine crabmeat, a half cup bread crumbs, mayonnaise, onions, chives, celery, red peppers, capers, parsley, zest, jerk sauce, pepper, nutmeg and egg. Form 12 crab cakes. Dredge in bread crumbs. Arrange on a platter, cover, and chill. Heat skillet with butter and oil. Brown crab cakes for 3-5 minutes on each side. Drain on paper towels. Serves 8.

☙

A tartar sauce dressing is my choicest crab cake dip, but substitutes are quite in order. Stuffed crab backs may be your preference. If so, try making some with the above mixture. Omit the eggs and bread crumbs. Fill crab backs. Top with a light sprinkling of bread crumbs and a dot of butter. Bake in a 325° F oven for 10 minutes to a light golden brown. Happy crabbing!

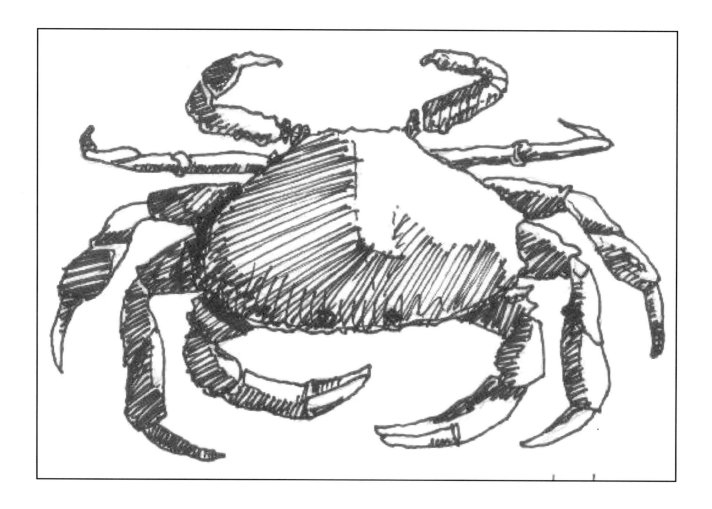

Fire Up Your Nuts

2   12-oz. pkg. almonds, macadamias, or pecans

2   tbsp. butter, melted

1   tbsp. cayenne pepper

1   tbsp. light soy sauce

1   tsp. ginger rice vinegar

1   tbsp. sugar or Splenda

Fire up the oven at 350° F. In a bowl, toss the almonds, macadamia nuts, or pecans with the butter, cayenne pepper, soy sauce, vinegar, and sugar. Lay out the mixture on a cookie sheet; stick it in the oven for 15 minutes and crackle up those nuts.

CSCS

These are only some of the suggested nuts to use, but whatever your heart's desire, any nut will work.

Guacamole or Avocado Dip

1 large ripe avocado

1 lime or lemon, juiced

2 cloves garlic, minced

2 stalks escallion (green onion) or green onions, sliced

4 plum tomatoes, minced

2 scotch bonnet peppers, minced (seeds removed)

1 red sweet pepper, minced

Salt and black pepper to taste

Peel and scoop avocado into a bowl. Add lime or lemon juice, minced garlic, green onions, tomatoes, peppers, salt, and pepper. Mash with a fork to combine all the ingredients, leaving a few chunky pieces of avocado in the mix. Serves 8.

☙

Serve as a dip with corn chips or crackers, or as a vegetable salad.

Jerk Pork Chunks

4   lbs. lean pork

4   tbsp. Baronhall Farms Jamaican dried jerk seasoning

2   tbsp. Baronhall Farms Jamaican scotch bonnet pepper sauce

1   tsp. Baronhall Farms Jamaican ground ginger

1   tsp. Baronhall Farms Jamaican ground allspice (pimento)

4   tbsp. lime or lemon juice

2   tbsp. rum or sherry

1   tbsp. garlic, finely chopped

1   large onion, finely chopped

Garnish with avocados, papayas and green allspice (pimento) leaves

Cut meat into 3-inch chunks, large enough to fit on a barbecue grill without falling through. Rub the jerk seasoning, ginger, allspice, lime or lemon juice, sherry or rum, garlic, and onion into the meat; cover and marinate for 24 hours in the refrigerator. Barbecue meat on a slow fire, approximately 4–6 inches away from hot coals. For a more exotic taste, place a few pimento leaves on top of the meat while cooking. Cover the grill to allow the gentle smoke flavor to penetrate. Turn meat at five-minute intervals to prevent burning. Cook until meat is no longer pink, but rich, deep brown in color. Arrange on a platter and decorate with your favorite fruit, vegetable, or a sprig of fresh green pimento leaves.

 CB

Crispy, hot, spicy chunks are ready to be devoured! Remember, if you cannot handle the heat, reduce the pepper…what goes in must come out—this could hurt you twice!

Oysters to the Rescue

2   dozen fresh, live oysters

1   cup ginger wine vinegar

1   tbsp. sugar

½   tsp. light soy sauce

1   clove garlic, minced

¼   tsp. Baronhall Farms Jamaican Hell Hot pepper sauce

2   lemons, wedges

Shucking oysters is no easy chore, but if you choose to do it yourself, wash and scrub them well to get rid of any dirt, sand, or muck. Use a strong, sharp knife to pry open. You may ask to have your oysters washed and shucked at the time of purchase, and ask for the shells. Keep refrigerated no more than a couple hours, or plan to serve them right away. Re-arrange the oysters on the shells and place on a platter with crushed ice beneath. Place a dish in the center of the platter with a mixture of ginger wine vinegar, sugar, soy sauce, garlic, and hell-hot sauce. Decorate with lemon wedges.

☙

Take a hint … an aphrodisiac of this caliber may be your Viagra replacement. You will need it for the shucking long ride—from Necking in Haulover to Naked City in Copulation, with no rest stops before your return trip via Ackendown to Speculation!

Pan-Curled Oysters

1   stick butter

1   tbsp. paprika

1   tsp. seasoning salt

1   tsp. light soy sauce

1   cup clam juice

48 oysters, washed and shucked (save the juice)

1   tsp. Baronhall Farms Jamaican Hell Hot pepper sauce

3   cups half and half milk

    Serve hot

8   serving bowls

8   slices of French bread, toasted

1   small bunch of chives, minced

1   tsp. paprika

In a non-stick saucepan, combine 4 tablespoons butter, paprika, seasoning salt, soy sauce, and clam juice. Heat on medium high, until the butter has melted, about one to two minutes. Reduce heat to medium. Add oysters and juice. Cook until the oysters curl at the edges, about two minutes. Add the hell-hot sauce, the half and half, and bring almost to a boil. Remove from heat and serve hot. Place a slice of toast in each bowl; pour the oysters over the toast, sprinkle with chives, a dash of paprika, and a dollop of butter. Serves 8.

ೞ

Sop it up as an appeteaser or any way you wish—it hits the spot anyway.

Patties (Jamaican Meat Pies)

Pastry

4	cups flour	1	cup beef suet (fat)
1	tsp. salt	½	cup vegetable shortening
1	tsp. baking powder	1	cup ice water
1	tsp. turmeric or saffron		

Mix flour, salt, baking powder, and turmeric or saffron together. Gradually cut in suet and shortening. Add water slowly, mixing with a fork until dough comes together, leaving the bowl clean. Dough should not be crumbly. Store in the freezer or refrigerate to chill. Divide to make 20 regular or 40 cocktail sized patties. Form into balls. Set aside.

Filling

2	lbs. ground beef	1	tsp. ginger, minced or grated
1	tsp. soy sauce (for color)	½	tsp. seasoning salt or plain salt
4	sprigs thyme or 2 tsp. thyme leaves	1	tsp. sugar (to taste)
4	stalks escallion (green onion), chopped finely	1	cup bread crumbs
2	onions, chopped finely	1	tbsp. butter
2	scotch bonnet peppers, minced	1	tbsp. oil (for glazing)

Season meat with soy sauce, thyme, escallion (green onion), onion, pepper, and ginger. Heat skillet with oil and cook meat until tender, about 30 minutes. Add seasoning salt, sugar, bread crumbs, butter, and water if necessary. Stir to combine and bring to a smooth, moist, but not runny consistency. Turn off heat. Cool before making patties. On a floured board, roll out dough balls into circles. Place 2–3 tablespoons of the meat mixture into the center of each circle. Fold in half. Use a fork to crimp the edges. Brush with oil. Bake at 350° F for 35–40 minutes or until golden brown. Makes 20–40.

ঙ্গ

Patties to Jamaicans are like hamburgers to Americans, or fish and chips to the English. Serve them hot and spicy like nine-day love!

Pepper Shrimps

3   lbs. freshly washed shrimps

¼   cup canola oil

1   tbsp. butter

3   cloves garlic, diced

2   tbsp. salt

3   whole peppers, minced

1   tbsp. vinegar

In a large Dutch pot or heavy skillet, heat the oil. Then add the butter and garlic. Add the shrimps and pepper. Parch and stir, cooking until shrimps are orange-pink in color. Remove from heat. Serves 4.

ଔ

Pepper shrimps as hot as fire—let me make you aware!

Pepper hypes your desire—but have no fear!

It gets to your fingers—among other things!

So wash before it lingers—go ahead, spread your wings!

Quiche

Pastry

2 cups flour, sifted	½ cup butter
1 pinch salt	2 egg yolks

In a bowl, mix the flour, salt, butter, egg yolks, and just enough water to bind the pastry crust. Roll out and line one 9-inch ovenproof pie dish. Bake at 450° F for 15 minutes. Lower the oven temperature to 325° F. Remove pastry shell from heat. Set aside.

Filling

4 eggs, beaten	2 cups cheese (Gruyere, Swiss, Cheddar), grated
1 pinch salt	8 slices bacon, chopped, fried crisp, drained
¼ tsp. cayenne pepper	1 cup escallion (green onion), or chives, chopped
2 cups cream, warmed	

Beat the eggs with salt, pepper, warmed cream, cheese, bacon, and half the green onions. Pour into the pastry shell. Return to the preheated oven and continue baking for about 30 minutes, or until the filling is firmly set. Garnish with chopped parsley, cilantro, or chives. Serves 8.

☙

Create some merry variations of your own. Some suggestions are cooked chicken, shrimp, ham, peas, spinach, and vegetables. Tomatoes are a no-no; the acidity will curdle the filling.

Salmon Balls

1   onion, minced

4   cloves garlic, minced

1   15oz. can salmon, drained

1   cup mashed potato

1   tsp. scotch bonnet pepper, minced

½   tsp. thyme leaves

¼   tsp. salt

1   egg, lightly beaten

¼   cup flour, for dusting fish balls

1   cup canola oil

Cilantro or chives for decorating

In a bowl, combine onion, garlic, drained salmon, mashed potatoes, pepper, thyme, salt, and egg. The batter will be sticky but thick enough to roll into balls. Roll about a spoonful of batter in both hands; dip lightly in flour. Heat oil in a deep, heavy-duty frying pan. Deep-fry balls until brown all around. Drain on paper towels. Arrange on a serving platter. Decorate with cilantro or chives. Serve with a tartar sauce or another dip of choice. Serves 8.

ଔ

Are you out of sauces? Go for a "quickie." Using the food processor, puree any leftover tomatoes, onion, garlic, vinegar, or lemon juice, olive oil, and a dash of salt and pepper to taste.

Salt and Pepper Beef Ribs

16   short ribs (cut crosswise)

2   tbsp. lemon juice

1   tsp. garlic powder

2   tbsp. salt

1   tsp. Baronhall Farms Jamaican scotch bonnet pepper powder

1   cup shredded cabbage

2   jalapeño peppers, sliced

Have your butcher cut the short ribs in thin crosscut slices. Season the ribs with lemon juice, garlic, salt, and pepper. Leave to marinate for 30 minutes. Grill for a minute on each side. Decorate platter with shredded cabbage and slices of jalapeño pepper. Lay slices of barbecued salt-and-pepper ribs on top. Serves 8.

☘

Serve as an appeteaser and provide little toothpicks to stick 'em up! Incidentally, try other cuts of meat or shellfish. Shrimp fare exceptionally well when prepared this way.

Sips 'n Bites

Soups:

To give your soups a lift, try garnishing with some slivered almonds, four-inch blades of chives, escallion (green onion) flowers, dollops of sour cream, grated cheese, radish strips, chopped parsley, celery or cilantro, lemon zest, crackers, croutons, or freshly toasted breadcrumbs. Like works of art that require hours of preparation before an exhibition, your soups may be fit for gala events, enough to cause a stir, with some serious salivating.

Most of the ingredients used in the preparation of these soups, and many other recipes in this book, are found mainly in Jamaican markets and supermarkets. However, if you're not a native there, have no fear! You will find a variety of condiments, spices, fruits, agricultural products, cocos, yams, and more, in any number of West Indian, Hispanic, Asian, and gourmet or specialty markets around the globe. Better yet, take a trip to Jamaica. The airports and seaports boast many shops. The Coffee Shop located in the Donald Sangster International Airport in Montego Bay, Jamaica, is one of the many shops from which to purchase your specialty items. I dare you to visit the Island, where you'll luxuriate—maybe play some golf, or take in some other attractions. But remember not to leave without your Blue Mountain Jamaica Coffee, or your Baronhall Farms coffee, spices and condiments. Check them out!

Bak Cjam Gai or Chinese Cock Soup	Mannish Water or Goat Soup
Beef Cilantro Soup	Onion Soup
Beef Pumpkin Soup	Oxtail Soup
Conch Soup	Pepperpot Callaloo Soup
Cow-Cod Soup	Red Peas Soup
Ginger Wine Soup	Seafood Shrimp Gumbo
Gungo Peas Soup	

Bak Cjam Gai or Chinese Cock Soup

1   4-lb. young cock chicken

1   corned or preserved turnip, washed and sliced

10 cups water

salt to taste

6   cloves garlic, minced

1   whole onion, peeled

1   tsp. fresh ginger, crushed

2   carrots, diced

1   cho-cho or chayote squash, sliced

1   corned turnip, washed and sliced

1   scotch bonnet pepper, diced (discard seeds)

3   stalks escallion (green onion), chopped

In a large stockpot, bring water and turnip to a rolling boil. Add the cleaned whole chicken, cover, and return to a boil. Remove the chicken, add some salt and ginger on the inside cavity, and set aside. When the water boils again, return the chicken to the pot with the garlic, onion, and ginger. Cover and simmer for 5 minutes. Turn off the heat and leave to steep for one hour. Remove chicken to a cutting board and carve into bite-sized pieces, then arrange on a platter. Return the pot to a boil. Add the carrots, cho-cho, turnip, and pepper. Simmer for 20 minutes, until all the vegetables are cooked. Add some chopped escallion (green onion). Serves 8.

☙

Make a garlic sauce to serve with the chicken:

Heat 2 tablespoons of canola oil, and stir in 2 cloves of minced garlic. While sizzling, pour over 2 tablespoons of soy sauce and 2 tablespoons of minced escallion (green onion), directly into the sauce dish. For a hot and spicy alternative, try the garlic-ginger-pepper or dipping sauce in "Dip It."

Beef Cilantro Soup

8   cups beef broth

¼   lb. ground round

2   cloves garlic, minced

¼   cup fresh or canned straw mushrooms, sliced

2   tsp. cornstarch or gravy flour

¼   cup cold water

1   egg white, lightly beaten

4   stalks escallion (green onion), make flowers

1   bunch cilantro, chopped

In a saucepan, bring broth to a boil. Add the ground beef, garlic, ginger, escallion (green onion) and mushrooms. Simmer for two to three minutes. Add the mixture of cornstarch and cold water. Return to a boil. Remove from heat. Gradually whisk in the lightly beaten egg white. Garnish with escallion (green onion) flowers and cilantro. Serves 8.

℞

Variations may be made to satisfy individual tastes. Instead of beef, try chicken, seafood, fish, or tofu.

Beef Pumpkin Soup

2	lbs. beef shank		3	sprigs thyme
1	lb. salt beef (soaked overnight to remove excess salt)		1	cho-cho (chayote squash), diced
1	whole onion		2	turnips, diced
3	lbs. yellow pumpkin, diced		2	carrots, diced
6	slices yellow yam		4	stalks escallion (green onion)
3	cups flour (make 12—see dumplings)		2	cloves garlic, chopped finely
3	Irish potatoes, quartered		1	packet chicken noodle or cock soup mix
4	ears corn on the cob, quartered or halved		2	slices fresh ginger
1	whole green scotch bonnet pepper		6	grains Baronhall Farms Jamaican pimento (allspice)

In an 8-quart stockpot, bring 3 quarts of water to boil. Add beef shanks and salt beef and onion. Cook for about 40 minutes until meat is almost tender. Add pumpkin, yam, dumplings, potatoes, corn, whole pepper, and thyme. Continue cooking for 10 minutes, and then add cho-cho, turnips, carrots, escallion (green onion), garlic, cock soup mix, ginger, and allspice grains. Simmer until everything is fully cooked. Taste for flavour, adding more seasonings if desired. Before serving the soup, be sure to remove and discard the whole pepper, onion, thyme stems, escallion (green onion), ginger, and allspice (pimento) grains. Serves 8.

❧

Servings are hearty and include as much food as one can consume in one sitting. It's Saturday's traditional one-pot meal. Bring the family together—gorge yourself! Expect a "belly full."

Conch Soup

3-4 lbs. fresh conch, cleaned

2   lemons, juiced

12 cups water

2   cups carrots and cho-cho or chayote squash, diced

3   Irish potatoes and coco, peeled and diced (coco is a starchy tuber like yam)

3   sprigs thyme

1   scotch bonnet pepper, minced (seeds removed)

Salt to taste

3   stalks escallion (green onion), chopped for garnish

Wash the conch three times if necessary, to remove hidden grains of sand. Cut the conch into small pieces and place in a bowl with the lemon juice. Refrigerate for a couple of hours. Bring the water to a boil in a soup pot and add the marinated conch. Cover and cook on medium heat for about 2 hours. When meat is tender, add carrots, cho-cho, potatoes, coco, thyme, pepper and salt to taste. Simmer for another 30 minutes to cook the vegetables. Pour into individual soup cups and add garnish. Serves 8.

છ

Sound the conch shell … you've all done swell … waiting with eager lips … puckering for a few sips!

Cow Cod Soup

1	cow cod (penis), washed and cleaned with vinegar and water
4	quarts (16 cups) water
1	tsp. seasoning salt
2	scotch bonnet peppers, 1 minced (seeds removed)
½	cup garlic and onions, minced
2	cups each, pumpkin, cho-cho, and carrots, diced
4	slices yellow yam, dasheen or coco
4	sprigs thyme
12	pimento (allspice) berries+
4	stalks escallion (green onion), diced
2	limes or lemons, juiced

Dash of nutmeg or slivers of ginger

Wash the cow cod in vinegar and water. Trim off any hair, fat, or unwanted tissues. Cut into small pieces. In a pressure cooker, add water, cow-cod, salt, and pepper. Pressurize for one hour or until meat is tender. Skin any visible fat or scum. Add onions, garlic, pumpkin, cho-cho, carrots, yam, dasheen, thyme, and pimento. Simmer for 30 minutes. Add the escallion (green onion), lemon juice, nutmeg, and ginger. Discard the thyme stems and pimento grains. Serves 12.

 C3

Ye men! Talk about virility—this will put "lead in your pencil." Women, be careful what you ask for; you may get more than "vim in your voom."

Ginger Wine Soup

12 chicken wings, jointed

½ lb. ginger, peeled and minced

6 cloves garlic, minced

½ tsp. salt

6 cups tonic wine

2 cups water

In a non-reactive pot, parch the garlic, ginger, and chicken until lightly brown. Add the tonic wine or a sweet to medium-dry wine. Cover pot tightly and simmer on low heat for one hour. Serves 8.

03

In Jamaica, our Chinese parents always prepared this tonic soup with pigeons. They believed that it rebuilds energy, strength, and vitality for anyone feeling run-down, recovering from surgery, or for nursing mothers.

Gungo (Pigeon) Peas Soup

2   cups green gungo peas

8   cups water

1   lb. salt beef

1   lb. beef shank or stew

1   lb. gooseneck or ham bone (optional)

1   onion, chopped

3   stalks escallion (green onion), chopped

2   cloves garlic, minced

1   whole scotch bonnet pepper

2   sprigs thyme

7   grains Baronhall Farms Jamaican pimento (allspice)

2   lbs. yellow yam or yam of choice, peeled and sliced

12   dumplings (see Dumplings)

1   cho-cho or chayote squash, peeled and sliced

1   carrot, sliced

Wash peas and salt beef and place with beef shank, gooseneck, or ham bone, in a 4-quart pot with water. Bring to boil, skim foam. Lower heat, cover and simmer for 2 hours, or until meat and peas are tender. Add onion, escallion (green onion), garlic, pepper, thyme, allspice, yam, dumplings, cho-cho, and carrot. Cook on low heat until the food is soft. Carefully remove thyme stems, allspice grains, and the whole pepper. Stir and check consistency. If necessary, add water. Add some escallion (green onion) to the top of each serving. Serves 8.

03

Gungo peas, otherwise known as Congo or Pigeon peas, are most popular at Christmastime; so traditionally most Jamaican families relish their end-of-season gungo peas soup, made with leftover turkey or hambone. Either or, it's a savoury delight to the last drop!

Mannish Water or Goat Soup

5 lbs. ram goat tripe, head, and feet, cut into 1-inch or 2-inch pieces

½ cup vinegar

10 quarts water

12 young green bananas, diced with skin

1 lb. coco (a tuber like yam), cubed

4 Irish potatoes, peeled and cubed

1 lb. yellow yam, cubed

2 chayote squash (cho-cho), diced

4 large carrots, diced

1 lb. curry pumpkin, diced

1 cups finely chopped onions

3 tbsp. salt (less or more to taste)

12 grains Baronhall Farms allspice (pimento)

2 scotch bonnet peppers

1 finger of ginger, diced

4 tbsp. thyme leaves

1 cup finely chopped escallion (green onion)

3 dozens spinners (see recipe for Dumplings)

2 packets cock or chicken noodle soup (optional)

1 cup white rum (optional)

Wash the tripe in vinegar and water. Wash head and feet thoroughly. Bring tripe, head, and feet to boil in a large pot with water. Skim foam as it forms. Cook for 3 hours or until meat falls off the bones. Discard bones. Add green bananas, coco, potatoes, yam, cho-cho, carrots, pumpkin, onions, salt, pimento grains, scotch bonnet pepper, ginger, thyme, escallion (green onion), and spinners. Simmer uncovered for one hour. Add chicken noodle. Simmer until soup reaches a full-bodied consistency. Serve in heatproof cups. Serves 30.

CB

Mannish water, a hearty, sumptuous soup, renowned for its aphrodisiac properties and believed to "put it back," to "put lead in his pencil," to "mek a man bray like a donkey," and as the calypsonian, the Mighty Sparrow sings, "mannish water mek yuh daughta walk and talk."

Onion Soup

6   medium onions, sliced thinly into rings

5   tbsp. butter or canola oil

2   tbsp. flour

½   tsp. seasoning salt

1   tsp. sugar

¼   tsp. Baronhall Farms Jamaican dried scotch bonnet pepper

6   cups beef broth

1   cup wine, sherry and cognac

2   cups grated Swiss and Parmesan cheeses

6   ½" slices Jamaican hard dough bread, toasted

Heat butter or canola oil in a Dutch oven. Sauté onion rings until golden brown. Stir while sprinkling in the flour, salt, sugar, and pepper. Add beef broth and wine mixture. Bring to boil. Simmer slowly for half an hour. Toast bread and put aside. Preheat broiler. Sprinkle a thin layer of cheese in fireproof soup bowls. Pour soup in each bowl, leaving space to float a slice of toast on top. Sprinkle remaining cheese on toast. Place bowls in a large cookie sheet under the broiler until the cheese melts and forms a nice brown crust on top. Serves 6.

CB

Smile and the world smiles with you—as this bubbly soup puts a bubbly smile on your face!

Oxtail Soup

- 2 lbs. oxtail pieces
- 1 lb. salt beef
- 3 quarts water
- 1 lb. yellow yam, peeled and sliced
- 3 Irish potatoes, peeled and sliced
- 2 cup flour (16 dumplings, kneaded and set aside (see recipe for Dumplings)
- 2 large carrots, diced
- 1 chayote squash (cho-cho), sliced
- 1 whole scotch bonnet pepper
- 1-2 pieces of scotch bonnet pepper (seeds removed)
- 1 onion, diced
- 2 cloves garlic, diced
- 2 stalks escallion (green onion), diced
- 2 sprigs thyme or thyme leaves
- 6 grains Baronhall Farms Jamaican pimento (allspice)

In a four-quart pot, place the oxtail, salt beef, and water, and bring to a boil. Cook for about two hours, or for 25 minutes in a pressure cooker. Meat should be tender but not falling off the bones. Add yam, potatoes, flour dumplings, carrots, cho-cho, pepper, onion, garlic, escallion, thyme, and allspice. Bring to a boil, reduce heat to medium-low, simmering for about 20 minutes, until everything comes into its own with a full-bodied consistency. At this time, remove the whole pepper, thyme stems, and allspice grains. Sprinkle some diced escallion, or chives in each bowl and serve soup while hot. Serves 8.

Wide-rimmed bowls or dainty mugs, filled to the brim with this gummous soup—decked with all the goodies, trimmings, and accessories—once devoured, will leave tell-tale signs that something hit the spot, and sealed each lip with a kiss!

Pepperpot Callaloo Soup

8-10 cups water

1 lb. beef stew or beef shin

1 lb. salt beef, soaked overnight

1 lb. shrimp, shelled and deveined (optional)

1 cup callaloo (Jamaican type of spinach), steamed and chopped

1 cup spinach, steamed and chopped

1 cup okra, diced

1 cup Indian kale, diced

1 medium-sized dasheen or coco, peeled and diced

1 lb. yellow yam, peeled and diced

1 medium carrot, diced

1 medium onion, finely chopped

4 cloves garlic, finely chopped

4 stalks escallion (green onion), diced

4 sprigs thyme

½ tsp. Baronhall Farms Jamaican scotch bonnet pepper

1 whole green scotch bonnet pepper

8 grains Baronhall Farms Jamaican allspice (pimento)

1 cup coconut milk

1 cup flour for spinners or dumplings (see recipe for Dumplings)

Bring water to a rolling boil in a six-quart soup pot. Add beef (stew, shin, and salt beef) and cook until tender. Add callaloo, spinach, okra, kale, dasheen, yam, and carrot. Continue cooking for 30 minutes more. Add dumplings or spinners, onion, garlic, escallion, thyme, pepper, pimento grains, and coconut milk. Lower heat and simmer for 20 minutes. Remove and discard the pimento grains, thyme stems and whole pepper. Serve soup while hot—as a one-pot meal. Add shrimps during the last five minutes of the cooking time. May be served with wedges of baked cassava bammies, or any favorite bread. Serves 8.

ଔ

Pepperpot, as the name indicates, is a pot of gumbo-based soup, highly spiced and peppered, having callaloo, kale, spinach and okra as the main vegetable ingredients.

Red Peas Soup

3   cups red kidney beans (peas)

3   quarts water

2   lb. beef shank

1   lb. salt beef

6   slices green breadfruit (when in season)

2   medium cocos or malanga (a starchy tuber like yam), peeled and sliced

4   yellow yam, slices

8   cornmeal dumplings

3   stalks escallion (green onion), chopped

3   sprigs thyme

1   scotch bonnet pepper, whole

1   pepper, minced (discard seeds)

6   grains Baronhall Farms Jamaican allspice (pimento)

Garnish with blades of chives or chopped escallion (green onion)

In a large soup pot, bring beans, water, and beef to a full boil for 30 minutes. Skim off any foam. Add slices of breadfruit, yam, and cornmeal dumplings, escallion, thyme, pepper, and pimento grains. Continue cooking until peas and meats are tender. Add more seasonings, if necessary. Remove and discard the whole pepper, thyme stems, and pimento grains. Puree in a blender 4 cups of the soup and peas. Return to the soup pot. Get ready to serve this as a full meal. Garnish each soup bowl with a few blades of chives or chopped escallion. Serves 8.

⍅

Get ready for a hearty, full-of-goodness, one-pot meal; a soup that may make you feel like you bit off more than you can chew!

Seafood Shrimp Gumbo

3	tbsp. butter	2	cups broth or water
4	small leeks, trimmed, washed, and sliced thinly	4	potatoes, peeled and cubed
1	cup okra, washed and sliced	1	cup heavy cream
1	cup onion, garlic, pepper, and thyme leaves, chopped	1	lb. large shrimp, peeled and deveined
1	scotch bonnet pepper, minced, seeds removed	1	lb. snapper fillet, cubed
1	cup tomatoes, pureed	1	lb. scallops, halved
4	cups clam juice	1	packet hot and spicy soup mix

3 tbsp. butter

4 small leeks, trimmed, washed, and sliced thinly

1 cup okra, washed and sliced

1 cup onion, garlic, pepper, and thyme leaves, chopped

1 scotch bonnet pepper, minced, seeds removed

1 cup tomatoes, pureed

4 cups clam juice

2 cups broth or water

4 potatoes, peeled and cubed

1 cup heavy cream

1 lb. large shrimp, peeled and deveined

1 lb. snapper fillet, cubed

1 lb. scallops, halved

1 packet hot and spicy soup mix

Unsalted water crackers

3 stalks escallion (green onion), or chives, diced

In a large soup pot, melt butter. Sauté the leeks, okra, onion, garlic, thyme, and pepper. Add tomatoes, clam juice, broth, water, and potatoes. Bring to boil. Add cream, shrimps, snapper, and scallops; allow simmering. Gradually add packet of soup mix, stirring to dissolve. Taste and add salt if needed. Cover and continue to simmer for 10–15 minutes, until shrimps are pink and the fish and scallops are fully cooked. Serves 8.

ಞ

Pop out some crackers on the side. Garnish each serving of gumbo with escallion (green onion) or chives.

Sips 'n Bites

Salads:

There are recipes in this book requiring the use of "Ackee," and, for those who are unfamiliar with the product, who may have heard that ackee is poisonous, here's a briefing on the subject, that hopefully will allay your fears. Ackee is consumed in Jamaica, and has gone worldwide. Tourists and visitors to the island have come to love "ackee and saltfish," which is popularly known as Jamaica's national dish. The Agricultural and Food authorities of Jamaica have strict guidelines for the safe handling and processing of Ackee for export. Hence, if bought in cans from the grocer, it is considered safe for the consumer.

Ackee grows like a fruit on a tree, and due to the combined ways in which it is cooked and eaten, it is classified as a vegetable, but I'd say, it may easily be categorized as a vegetarian kind of meat. When cooked, ackee looks very similar to scrambled eggs, and it is very tasty too. However, there is a poisonous gas inside the pale green, immature fruit pod. But, as it matures, the pod changes to a bright reddish-orange color. In time, the fruit ripens and bursts open, automatically releasing the gas; exposing three pieces of buttery-yellow fruit, each with a black seed and a red vein lining inside. The seed and vein must be removed and discarded prior to preparation for cooking. Ackee is an edible fruit.

This book boasts many recipes, and a "Spicy Pocket Dictionary" with briefs—tales—tips, some about our Island foods and spices. There is also a picture of ackee, before it is cooked, as it is sold locally. Check out this chapter, "picture, no picture – yes, picture."

Breadfruit Ackee Salad	Macaroni Potato Salad
Caesar Salad	Old-fashioned Coleslaw
Coconut Coleslaw	Oriental Cucumber Pepper Salad
Coleslaw My Way	Salted Codfish Salad
Crushed Nuts Chicken Salad	String Bean Garlic Pepper Salad
Guacamole Mound	Vegetarian Bean Casserole
	Waldorf Salad with Chicken

Breadfruit Ackee Salad

2   cups breadfruit, boiled, drained

1   can Ackee (2 cups cooked) drained

4   hard-boiled eggs, peeled, diced

1   large onion, minced

1   tbsp. garlic, minced

2   tbsp. Italian dressing or mayonnaise

1   bunch chives, chopped

1   tbsp. red sweet pepper, minced

Now that the breadfruit, ackee, and eggs are already cooked, drained and diced, combine in a salad bowl. Gently toss with the garlic, onion, salad dressing or mayonnaise. Garnish with paprika, cayenne pepper, chives, and minced red sweet pepper. Chill. Serves 8.

ᴄᴈ

The green breadfruit is boiled for use in this dish and may be served chilled. However, the roasted breadfruit may also be used, but is best when served warm. Enjoy whatever variety you wish—you've come a long way, babe!

Caesar Salad

2   filets of anchovies

3   cloves garlic, minced

1/2 tsp. ground pepper

1   tbsp. lemon juice

1   tbsp. white balsamic vinegar

1   tsp. Worcestershire sauce

1   tsp. Dijon mustard

½   cup extra virgin olive oil

3   bunches romaine, washed and drained

½   cup toasted herb croutons

Freshly ground black pepper

½   cup grated Parmesan cheese

Break lettuce into bite-sized pieces and set aside. In a salad bowl, mash to a paste the anchovies, garlic, pepper, lemon juice, vinegar, Worcestershire sauce, and Dijon mustard. Briskly whisk in the olive oil. Add lettuce and croutons. Toss gently. Serve in individual salad bowls with freshly ground pepper and a sprinkle of cheese on top. Serves 8.

ख

For health reasons, raw eggs and extra salt may be replaced with anchovies.

Coconut Coleslaw

½ cup low-fat mayonnaise dressing

¼ cup low-fat sour cream

1 tsp. honey mustard

1 tsp. garlic paste

1 tbsp. freshly squeezed lemon juice

1 tbsp. cider vinegar

1 tbsp. sugar

¼ tsp. salt

1 dash Baronhall Farms Jamaican ground scotch bonnet pepper

2 cups finely shredded coconut

4 cups finely shredded cabbage

¾ cup shredded carrot

¼ cup seedless raisins

8 radishes: make roses and leave in ice water

1 bunch watercress, washed and drained

Combine mayonnaise, sour cream, honey mustard, garlic paste, lemon juice, vinegar, sugar, salt, and pepper. Chill. Toss together in a large salad bowl the shredded coconut, cabbage, carrot, raisins, and the mayonnaise combination. Decorate with the radish roses and watercress. Serve chilled. Treat yourself to this Caribbean-style coleslaw.

௸

Have a crack at the coconut; take a hammer to it; save the meat for shredding and experience its nutty goodness!

Coleslaw My Way

1 head green cabbage, shredded

½ head purple cabbage, shredded

2 carrots, shredded

2 sweet peppers, red and yellow: julienne

1 onion, chopped finely

1 lemon, juice extracted

½ cup granulated sugar

1 cup white vinegar

¼ cup canola oil

1 tsp. mustard

1 tsp. salt

1 tsp. cayenne pepper

1 tsp. lemon zest

In a large bowl, combine cabbage, carrot, sweet peppers, onion, and lemon juice. Sprinkle with sugar and set aside. In a saucepan, combine vinegar, oil, mustard, salt, and pepper. Bring to a boil. Pour over cabbage. Stir. Cool. Stir again to combine. Cover. Refrigerate for a few hours before serving. Serves 12.

 C3

A salad of this nature may be dressed up or down—the added red or yellow sweet peppers make a more attractive presentation—the zest adds spunk to your salad.

Crushed Nuts Chicken Salad

4   cups cooked chicken breast, diced

¼   tsp. garlic powder

4   cups seedless grapes

1   cup crushed pineapple

1   cup apples, cubed

1   cup crushed walnuts or cashew nuts

1   tbsp. lime or lemon juice

1   tbsp. sugar

1/8 tsp. Baronhall Farms Jamaican ground nutmeg

½   tsp. Baronhall Farms Jamaican scotch bonnet hot sauce

1 ½cups Miracle Whip salad dressing

In a large salad bowl, toss together the diced chicken breast, some garlic or garlic powder, seedless grapes, pineapple, apples, walnuts, lemon juice, sugar, nutmeg, pepper sauce, and dressing. Chill. Serve on a bed of watercress or lettuce leaves, with hot dinner rolls or your favorite loaf of bread. This summertime favorite serves 8.

ୟ

Hurry up … pass it round, man … we are hungry bad!

Guacamole Mound

4 small avocados, halved and pitted

8 leaves frilly lettuce

1 cup purple lettuce, shredded

1 can albacore tuna, drained

24 medium shrimps, peeled, deveined, and cooked

4 radishes, sliced

3 stalks escallion (green onion), sliced

4 tbsp. creamy ranch dressing

Salt and pepper to taste

1 bunch cilantro, chopped

Arrange 8 salad bowls with lettuce, shredded cabbage, avocado halves, filled with a mixture of tuna, shrimps, radishes, escallion (green onion), ranch dressing, and a dash of salt and pepper. Serves 8.

ଔ

Decorate with chopped cilantro.

Macaroni Potato Salad

2   cups macaroni, cooked

4   potatoes, diced, cooked

1   medium onion, minced

1   cups carrots, cooked, drained

6   hard-boiled eggs, peeled, diced

Salt and pepper to taste

2   stalks celery, chopped

1   red bell pepper, chopped

4   lettuce leaves, broken in chunks

¼   cup Italian dressing or mayonnaise

Garnish with paprika and chives.

In a serving salad bowl, combine and gently toss together the macaroni, potatoes, minced onion, carrots, and hard-boiled eggs. Mash some of the eggs if desired. Chill for a couple hours. Add the chopped celery, pepper, and lettuce, and stir to incorporate the salad dressing or mayonnaise. Sprinkle the chives and paprika on top. Cover the bowl. Chill until serving time. Serves 8.

ଔ

Salads of this quality are my signature meals. They come in handy for those who are always on the run, too busy to cook every day. Plus, they are healthful, and honest to goodness, the best things since sliced bread.

Old-fashioned Coleslaw

1   head cabbage, shredded

1   carrot, shredded

1   onion, chopped finely

½   cup granulated sugar

1   cup white vinegar

¼   cup canola oil

1   tsp. mustard

1   tsp. salt

1   tsp. cayenne pepper

In a large bowl, combine cabbage, carrot, and onion. Sprinkle with sugar and let sit for a few minutes. In a saucepan, combine vinegar, oil, mustard, salt, and pepper. Bring to a boil. Pour over cabbage and stir to combine. Allow to cool, stir again. Cover and refrigerate for a few hours before serving as a salad. Serves 12.

ങ

To make this salad more attractive, red sweet peppers or more carrots may be added.

Oriental Cucumber Pepper Salad

2   large cucumbers

2   sweet red and yellow peppers

2   tsp. salt

1   clove garlic, minced

½   tsp. ginger, minced or pickled

¼   tsp. cayenne pepper

¼   tsp. Baronhall Farms Jamaican Hell Hot pepper sauce

1   tsp. sugar or equivalent amount of non-sugar sweetener

1   tbsp. apple cider vinegar

1   tsp. virgin olive oil

Score cucumbers, cut in four pieces lengthwise, then remove and discard seeds. Cut into diagonal slices, about 2 inches long. Repeat the same process for the sweet peppers. Place cucumber and pepper in a bowl with salt and leave for 10 minutes. Rinse away the excess salt, and drain. In the same bowl, add garlic, ginger, pepper, sugar, vinegar, and oil. Stir once. Cover and refrigerate. Serves 8.

෮

This colorful salad will retain its crispness for a few hours. Serve with steaks, fish, or any meat dish.

Salted Codfish Salad

1   lb. salted codfish

4   plum tomatoes, diced

1   red sweet pepper, minced, no seeds

1   scotch bonnet pepper, minced, no seeds

1   large cucumber, diced, no seeds

1   onion, minced

2   stalks celery or cilantro, chopped

2   tbsp. apple cider vinegar or lemon juice

3   tbsp. extra virgin olive oil

Dash of black pepper

Soak the salted fish overnight. Remove any bones. Flake the fish in a salad bowl. Add tomatoes, peppers, cucumber, onion, celery, cilantro, vinegar, and oil. Toss together well. Add a dash of black pepper. It is a colorful salad, but garnish if you wish. Serves 8.

⊗

Hard cracker or hard dough bread are popular accompaniments, but try it with fried breadfruit or fried green plantains. Remember, necessity is the mother of invention, so anything goes!

String Bean Garlic Pepper Salad

2	tbsp. canola or olive oil
3	cloves garlic, minced
1	lb. string beans, stems removed
1	tbsp. butter
1	tbsp. water
1	onion, diced
3	red, yellow sweet bell peppers, thinly sliced
2	sprigs escallion (green onion), flowers
1	teaspoon salt and pepper to taste

Heat wok on medium heat. Heat oil. Add garlic, string beans, butter, and only a tablespoon of water. Cover and steam for a few minutes. Remove cover. Add onion, peppers, green onion, salt, and pepper to taste. Stir-fry for 2 minutes and transfer to a serving dish immediately. Veggies will retain their crispy texture when prepared this way. Serves 8.

⊘

A colorful array of vegetables—stir-fried or steamed, are healthy and palatable combinations that qualify as a salad, and focuses on the daily dietary requirements. Of course, variety is the spice of life, so freely substitute and change combinations to match your taste or mood.

Vegetarian Bean Casserole

1	15 oz. can northern white beans
1	15 oz. can butter beans
1	15 oz. can baked beans
1	15 oz. can kidney beans
¼	teaspoon vinegar
1	onion, diced finely
1	sweet pepper, chopped
¼	tsp. Baronhall Farms Jamaican Hell Hot pepper sauce
4	tbsp. barbecue sauce
¼	tsp. Baronhall Farms Jamaican ground nutmeg
¼	tsp. Baronhall Farms Jamaican ground ginger
1	tbsp. brown sugar

Mix together the beans, vinegar, onion, pepper, pepper sauce, and barbecue sauce. Place in a lightly greased casserole dish and sprinkle the top with a mixture of nutmeg, ginger, and brown sugar. Bake in a preheated oven at 350° F for 45 minutes. Serve with rice, noodles, or potatoes, and a salad. Serves 8.

ↁ

Beans are easily digestible if served with celery or cucumbers, so try this with our Oriental Cucumber Salad. Serve it hot or cold or as a side dish.

Waldorf Salad with Chicken

1   large Fuji or red delicious apple, diced

1   tbsp. lemon or lime juice

1   lb. diced cooked chicken breast

1   cup chopped celery

½   cup coarsely chopped walnuts

½   cup seedless raisins

1   dash Baronhall Farms Jamaican Hell Hot pepper

1   dash Baronhall Farms Jamaican ground ginger

1   cup green seedless grapes

2   cups cooked noodles or potatoes, cooled (optional)

1   cup low-fat mayonnaise or salad dressing

Dice the apple and sprinkle with lemon juice to prevent discoloration. In a large salad bowl, mix apple, chicken, celery, walnuts, raisins, pepper, and ginger. Stir in grapes. Add noodles or potatoes (remember, these are optional). Add mayonnaise or salad dressing. Chill for one hour prior to serving. Serves 8.

怓

How about this easy, nourishing one-dish meal for those hot summer days or evenings? A Waldorf salad of this caliber may help keep the blues away—it's comfort food!

Sips 'n Bites

Breads:

Airtight tins will keep breads or baked goods fresh for up to three days. Wrap tins in plastic or zip-lock bags to keep a little longer. Plastic containers absorb odors, but if baked items are wrapped in foil first, they will keep. Freezing is the best way of storing baked goods, but first wrap in heavy-duty foil, plastic wrap, or freezer bags. Slice breads or cakes before freezing and wrap closely to prevent air or moisture from getting trapped inside. Thaw at room temperature when ready to use.

Bread – Country Crust
Cornbread Muffin Flair
French Toast
Gingerbread
Handle Me Gently Dough
Journey (Johnny) Cakes
Mango Bread
Pomona Crackers
Scones for High Tea

Bread - Country Crust

3	cups bread flour
2	tsp. sugar
½	tsp. salt
1	packet active dry yeast
2	tbsp. canola or olive oil
1	cup warm water (130° F)
¼	cup cornmeal
1	egg white, beaten

In a large mixing bowl, combine flour, sugar, salt, and yeast. Add warm water and oil and mix thoroughly. Turn out the dough onto a lightly floured board. Knead with the heel of the hands for 15 minutes. Place dough in a lightly greased bowl and turn once over. Cover the bowl with a towel. Leave in a warm place to rise for 30 minutes. Sprinkle an ungreased baking sheet with cornmeal. Punch down the dough. Cover with the inverted bowl. Rest for 10 minutes. Now with both hands, lightly knead and shape dough into an oval loaf. Place shaped dough on the baking sheet, cover with a towel, and let it rise for 30 minutes. Preheat the oven to 350° F. The dough will be double in size. Make a few diagonal slashes on the top of the loaf and apply the egg white or water with a brush. Bake for 30 to 35 minutes.

ଓ

Test the loaf for doneness. If it sounds hollow when tapped lightly with the fingers, have your butter ready. Time to break bread!

Cornbread Muffin Flair

2½ cups flour (sifted)

¼ cup cornmeal

¼ cup oatmeal

2 tsp. baking powder

¼ tsp. salt

1 packet coconut milk

1 packet milk powder

2 cups sugar

1 tsp. freshly grated nutmeg

1 tsp. Baronhall Farms Jamaican mixed spice

2 tbsp. butter

2 eggs (lightly beaten)

1 tsp. vanilla

1 cup water

Blend flour, cornmeal, oatmeal, baking powder, salt, milk powder, sugar, nutmeg, and mixed spice. Add butter, lightly beaten eggs, vanilla, and water. Mix thoroughly and pour into a 12-inch round baking pan. Bake at 350° F for 45 minutes or until rich golden brown. Serves 8.

☙

This cornbread muffin is fluffy, crusty, and created with a different twist. Serve fresh out of the oven, or warm with marmalade, jam, or syrup. And for that extra twist, add your favorite nuts, chocolate, raisins, or craisins, and the list could go on.

French Toast

2   cups eggnog

½   tsp. nutmeg

½   tsp. cinnamon

1   tsp. vanilla extract

Salt, optional

10 slices (hard-dough) bread

1   tbsp. butter

Blend together the eggnog, nutmeg, cinnamon, vanilla, and salt to taste. Soak bread slices in the mixture to coat both sides. Toast on a heated griddle until both sides are golden brown. Serves 8.

 CB

Having a Sunday brunch—pull out the cherry preserves or marmalades and complement your French toast. A maple syrup topping is the accepted norm.

Gingerbread

2   eggs

½   cup butter, melted

½   cup molasses

1½ cups brown sugar

½   cup hot water

½   cup ginger, grated

2   cups flour

1½ tsp. baking powder

1   tsp. Baronhall Farms Jamaican mixed spice

Pinch of salt

Preheat oven to 350° F. Beat the eggs until smooth. Combine with melted butter, molasses, sugar, water, and grated ginger. In a large mixing bowl, sift together the flour, baking powder, mixed spice, and salt. Then incorporate the wet mixture with the dry ingredients to form a smooth batter. Pour mixture into a 9-inch loaf pan. Bake for 25 minutes or until tested for doneness, the tester comes out clean. Cool. Drizzle with cream icing of choice. Serves 8.

❧

Gingerbread gives a slice of warmth to any aching stomach, and the way to a man's heart is through his stomach … get to it, ladies—spice it up!

Handle Me Gently Dough

2   cups flour

1   tbsp. sugar

¾   tsp. salt

3   tsp. baking powder

5   tbsp. cold, firm unsalted butter

½   cup buttermilk

½   cup whipped cream

Preheat oven to 425° F. Measure and mix together flour, sugar, salt, and baking powder into a large bowl. Using a pastry blender or two knives, cut the butter into the flour until it forms crumbs. Add buttermilk and whipped cream, tossing the mixture to form the dough. Turn dough onto floured surface and knead lightly. Pat the dough to about ½-inch thickness. Cut biscuits with a 2-inch cookie cutter. Place about 2 inches apart, on an ungreased baking sheet. Bake until golden for 10–15 minutes. Makes 12.

 CB

Handle Me Gently Dough is a befitting name, especially associated with the creation of this flaky, whipped-cream biscuit, an undertaking mixed with love and handled with care.

Journey (Johnny) Cakes

3   cups sifted flour

2   tsp. baking powder

¼   tsp. salt

1   tbsp. sugar, optional

1   tbsp. butter or margarine

1   cup water

½   cup canola oil

With a fork, mix together the flour, baking powder, salt, sugar, and butter. Add enough water to form crumbly dough. Knead gently until dough is smooth, not sticky. Cut or break into about twelve to fifteen pieces. Roll into balls then flatten slightly. Heat oil on a medium fire. Fry Johnny cakes on all sides until golden brown. Reduce heat to low. Cover the pan and shuffle around on the low heat for a few minutes. The cakes will have steamed gently, resulting in a softer crust. Makes 12.

CB

Here's a tale of how "Johnny cake" got its name. In the lean old days, with so little money to spare, most families made fried dumplings for breakfast or for Johnny to take to work, school, and on long journeys. John or Johnny was also the most common name, hence, the nicknames, "journey cake," and "Johnny cake."

Mango Bread

2   cups flour

2   tsp. baking soda

½   tsp. salt

2   tsp. ground cinnamon

1   cup sugar

3   eggs

¼   cup honey

1   tsp. vanilla extract

½   cup canola oil

1   cup chopped walnuts

½   cup chopped raisins

3   cups chopped mangoes

Mix together the flour, baking soda, salt, cinnamon, and sugar. Make a well in mixing bowl and add well-beaten eggs, honey, vanilla, and oil. Mix together, adding walnuts, raisins, and mangoes. Pour into a greased and floured loaf or tube pan. Bake in a preheated oven at 325° F for approximately one hour.

03

Mango, the lustful fruit ... enjoy it any style! Bananas are also a fruit to reckon with, so try making banana bread when mangoes are scarce.

Pomona Crackers

2   cups flour, more for later

2   tsp. salt

2   tbsp. sugar

2   tbsp. butter

¼   cup shortening

¼   cup milk

¼   cup ice-cold water

Prepare two baking sheets, lining them with aluminum foil. In a mixing bowl, combine the flour, salt, and sugar. Cut in the butter and shortening to make a crumb-like dough. Slowly mix in the milk and water. The dough will come into its own, forming a ball. Preheat oven to 300° F. Remove dough to a floured surface. Sprinkle flour to reduce the stickiness. Now with a rolling pin, literally beat the dough, adding more flour, beating and folding. Repeat the beating process, until the dough is flat and smooth. Roll out to ¼-inch thick. Cut out 3-inch circles. Place rounds on the prepared sheets about an inch apart. Prick small holes in each cracker with a fork. Bake for 20 minutes at 300° F. Reduce heat to 250° F and bake for another 20 minutes. Check for doneness; the crackers will harden, the bottom will be golden, and the top will appear whitish-pink in color. Remove from heat.

CB

Offer your crackers with butter, jams and marmalade, or a platter of cheeses and cold cuts.

Scones for High Tea

2½ cups flour

½ cup sugar

3 tsp. baking powder

¼ tsp. baking soda

½ tsp. salt

¼ cup raisins

¼ cup butter

2 eggs, beaten

½ cup heavy cream

1 tsp. vanilla

1 8-oz. jar cherry preserves

1 cup powdered sugar

Sift together the flour, sugar, baking powder, baking soda, and salt. Add raisins. Using the fingertips, mix the butter with flour to form a crumb-like mixture. Add the beaten eggs, milk, and vanilla. Knead gently. Turn out the dough onto a floured surface. Shape into a ball then roll out into a circle over ½-inch thickness. Cut into wedges. Place on a cookie sheet. Brush scones with milk or water. Bake in preheated 350° F oven for 12 minutes. Make a glaze with a mixture of 1 cup powdered sugar and 3 tablespoons fruit juice to match the fruit topping. Serves 8.

ଔ

"High Tea," is a British custom, handed down by our ancestors, still practiced by a scattering few in Jamaica. Served as a late-afternoon tea, tempered with sandwiches, teacakes, or scones, one may opt to add a fruit topping or drizzle a fruit glaze over their scones. Once tried, this will become a must on your menu for other occasions.

Intercourse

Before one gets into the intercourse or entree phase of a meal, for starters, indulge in some appeteasers, cocktails, hors d'oeuvres, or finger foods—it's the foreplay to what may be laid out on the platter later. Appeteasers most definitely will whet the appetite and have one anticipating more. There's so much more … no need to rush. A mindset; a timely approach leading into a five-course meal; cocktails, appeteasers, sips and bites, intercourse, and maybe some decadent chocolate-filled stress relievers or desserts; the after-dinner dessert wine; they are all habit-forming. Grandfather always said habits are like a cable; we weave a thread of it every day, until it forms an iron chain, and finally we cannot break it. Better yet, if sitting down to a timely meal is classified as one of the good habits, then why not do it? Whip it up to a seven-course meal … Do It in the Kitchen!

Ackee and Saltfish
Beef with Preserved Mustard (Ngow Yuk Ham Choy)
Broasted Salmon
Brown-Baked Baldpate or Doves
Bust Ya Chops on a Rack of Lamb
Char Siu (Chinese Roast Pork)
Chicken a la Baron
Chicken with Mushrooms (Dtung Goo Gai)
Chinese Steamed Omelet
Corned Beef (Home Cured)
Cornish Hens Broasted with Shallots
Cow Foot and Butter Beans
Curried Chicken
Curried Goat
Curried Lobster

Dip 'n Fall Back (Run Down)
Flaming Red Sizzler (Beef Barbecue)
Fricasseed Chicken (Cluck-Cluck)
Fried Rice
Jerk Chicken
Nyam-a-licious Stewed Peas
Oxtail with Butter Beans
Oyster Stew
Pepper Steak (Hot and Spicy)
Polenta (Turn Cornmeal)
Roast Beef (Pot Roast)
Roasted Lemon-Herb Chicken
Shepherd's Pie
Shrimps in Thyme and Garlic Sauce
Steam-baked Snapper
Stuffed Meatloaf Roll
Susumber (Gully Beans) with Saltfish
Swedish Meatballs

Ackee and Saltfish

2	dozens fresh ackee or 2 cans ackee		4	stalks escallion (green onion), diced
1	lb. saltfish (salted codfish or bacalao)		1	scotch bonnet pepper, diced (discard seeds)
2-4	tbsp. canola oil		½	tsp. thyme leaves
2	cloves chopped garlic		¼	tsp. freshly ground black pepper
1	large onion, chopped or sliced		Garnish: 8 escallion (green onion) flowers and 8 fried bacon strips
2	plum tomatoes, chopped			

Note: In this book, there are two sections defining "Ackee," the Spicy Pocket Dictionary, and Salads.

Soak salted codfish in water overnight. Drain. Place fish in fresh water and bring to boil, uncovered. Drain, cool, flake fish, set aside. If fresh ackees are used, clean, remove and discard the seeds and red membranes. Add ackees to rapidly boiling water. Cook until tender to the touch of a fork. Drain, set aside. Heat canola oil in a frying pan. Sauté the garlic, onions, tomatoes, escallion, pepper, and thyme. Add flaked, salted codfish and gently stir in the cooked ackee. Simmer uncovered for 5-7 minutes, reducing any excess liquid. Transfer to a serving dish. Sprinkle with black pepper and garnish. A delectable combination with Johnny cakes, dumplings, roasted breadfruit, baked or fried plantains, and slices of avocado. Serves 8.

☃

Ah! Leftovers! A potion that gives meaning to the saying, "love is better the second time around." You'll feel the love! Try adding leftover ackee and saltfish to steamed rice for a sumptuous seasoned rice. Create some ackee and salt fish sandwiches—bite-sized will do the trick. Serve as appeteasers or hors d'oeuvres at luncheons, tea parties, or dinners. Assuredly, there are many reasons why Jamaica's National Dish is "Ackee and Saltfish."

Beef with Preserved Mustard (Ngow Yuk Ham Choy)

1½ lbs. rump or flank steak

1   tsp. ginger sherry

2   tbsp. gravy flour

¼   tsp. seasoning salt

3   preserved mustard leaves, cut diagonally

2   tbsp. canola or peanut oil

3   slices ginger, julienne

3   cloves garlic, minced

1   tbsp. black bean paste

Sesame oil, optional flavor

1   tsp. soy sauce

½   cup broth or water

Cut beef into thin diagonal slices while partly frozen. Add ginger sherry, a teaspoon of gravy flour, and seasoning salt. Wash the preserved mustard greens, cut into small diagonal pieces, and set aside. Heat skillet and a tablespoon of oil. Add ginger, garlic, bean paste, and beef. Stir-fry quickly, no longer than two or three minutes. Add mustard greens and a dash of sesame oil. Mix the remaining gravy flour with the soy sauce, broth, or water, and add to the meat. Stir long enough to coat the meat and thicken the sauce. Serves 8.

❦

Transfer to a serving dish and complement with rice.

Broasted Salmon

8   salmon filets

Salt and pepper to taste

2   tbsp. thyme leaves

4   cloves garlic, minced

1   tbsp. prepared mustard

½   cup dry white wine

4   tbsp. extra virgin olive oil

1   tbsp. lemon zest

2   lemons, sliced for garnish

Cover a cookie sheet or roasting pan with foil. Lay out the salmon filets on the foil. Add salt and pepper on all sides. In a food processor, blend to a fine glaze the thyme, garlic, mustard, white wine, and olive oil. Spread or brush the glaze over the salmon filets. Broil or roast on each side, for about 10 to 12 minutes. Transfer to a platter. Decorate with lemon zest, slices of lemon, or add a touch of your favorite oil, extra virgin olive oil, truffle oil, or almond oil. Serves 8.

છ

Oven broiled-roasted salmon—I call it "broasted" just for the fun of it. And, who said one could not enjoy a meal with outdoor imaginings, broasted indoors?

Brown-Baked Baldpate or Doves

12   baldpate doves, cleaned

2   limes, juiced

1   tsp. seasoning salt

½   tsp. black pepper

4   tbsp. canola oil

2   tbsp. butter

1   scotch bonnet pepper

2   tomatoes, chopped

3   cloves garlic, minced

1   onion, chopped

6   sprigs thyme

2   cups water, wine, or sherry

Wash and clean the birds thoroughly. Soak for a few hours in salt water and wash off the remaining dried blood, or remove any extra feathers. Cut birds in halves or prepare whole. Dry and rub in lime juice, salt, pepper, and half the oil. Heat a heavy skillet with remaining oil and butter. Brown birds on all sides and remove from skillet to a baking dish or a pressure cooker. In the skillet, stir-fry the pepper, tomatoes, garlic, onions, thyme, and water or wine. Pour over the birds. Bake at 400° F for about 45 minutes. To pressure-cook, the liquid must barely cover the birds. Time for 10 minutes after the cooker starts hissing. Remove from heat, and allow the pressure to fall before opening. Arrange the birds on a platter. Sprinkle with thyme leaves and sauce. Serves 8.

෮

Baked doves fare well with roasted breadfruit, baked plantains, and an avocado salad, or they may be served as an appeteaser.

Bust Ya Chops on a Rack of Lamb

8-16   rib lamb chops or rack of lamb

3   tbsp. canola or olive oil

1   cup yogurt

½   tsp. freshly ground black pepper

3   cloves garlic, finely diced

3   tsp. dried rosemary and 3 sprigs rosemary

3   sprigs thyme

1   tsp. salt or seasoned salt

2   lemons—8 slices or wedges

Preheat oven to 475° F. Coat the meat with oil, yogurt, black pepper, garlic, dried rosemary and thyme. Wrap in foil and allow at least one hour for marinating. Add salt just before roasting or grilling. To Roast: set foil with lamb, fat side up, in a roasting pan and place in preheated oven for 15 – 20 minutes, turning at half time—10 minutes. For grilling: place rack of lamb, fat side up, on a greased grill for 15 – 17 minutes, turning once after 10 minutes. Test for doneness – they cook quickly, so watch closely. Remove from heat, transfer to a warm platter and allow resting for 10 minutes before serving. Decorate with sprigs of rosemary, thyme and lemon slices or wedges. Serves 8.

ℛ

You may test the meat for doneness by feeling it with your fingers—medium cooked, has a springy touch and a juicy texture—well done, feels firm. Hey, it's your rack; feel it, touch it, fondle it.

Char Siu (Chinese Roast Pork)

5   lbs. pork tenderloin or shoulder cut in 2-inch-thick slices

2   tbsp. canola oil

2   tbsp. rum or ginger sherry

3   tbsp. soy sauce

3   cubes red soybean curd (lam wui)

2   tbsp. roast pork (char siu) seasoning mix

1   tbsp. sugar

½   tsp. Baronhall Farms Jamaican scotch bonnet pepper

½   tsp. Baronhall Farms Jamaican ground allspice (pimento)

½   tsp. freshly grated nutmeg

¼   tsp. freshly grated ginger

1   tsp. Chinese five-spice powder (ng heung fun)

Garnish with escallion flowers (see green onion flowers)

Blend oil, rum, sherry, soy sauce, red bean curd, char siu seasoning, sugar, pepper, allspice, and ginger to form a marinade. Rub mixture well into each slice of meat. Cover and refrigerate, marinating overnight. Set in a drip pan to bake for 30 minutes at 500° F, then 30 minutes at 400° F. Remove from oven. Carve when cool. Arrange on a platter and garnish with escallion (green onion) flowers or parsley. Serves 8.

CB

Within the Chinese circle in Jamaica, the traditional belief is that the pig roots for his food, and symbolically, when eaten, propels one into happiness and wealth. Roast Pork is always on the menu at house parties, grand functions, and especially at weddings.

Chicken a la Baron

6	lbs. whole chicken or 8 chicken breasts
2	tbsp. canola oil
1	tbsp. seasoning salt
1	tbsp. mushroom soy sauce
½	tsp. scotch bonnet pepper
½	tsp. ginger, chopped finely
1	lime or lemon, sliced
8	whole garlic cloves
1	tsp. thyme leaves
2	stalks escallion (green onion), chopped
2	tbsp. butter or margarine
½	cup cognac or fruit juice
½	cup Baronhall Estate Jamaican coffee liqueur

Preheat oven to 500° F. Wash chicken and pat dry. Rub inside and out with oil, seasoning salt, soy sauce, pepper, and ginger. Heat heavy-duty skillet, brown chicken on all sides, and remove to a roasting pan. Stuff the chicken cavity with the lemon slices, garlic, thyme, escallion, and butter. Roast whole chicken for about 50 minutes, 40 minutes for chicken breasts. Transfer chicken to a platter. Add cognac or fruit juice and coffee liqueur to the pan drippings in the skillet, and bring to a boil, reducing the sauce. Pour over the chicken or serve in a gravy boat on the side.

ෞ

Talk about nice like a pound of rice! Ahy yha yhai!

Chicken with Mushrooms (Dtung Goo Gai)

6	chicken drumsticks	1	tbsp. peanut or canola oil
3	chicken breasts	1	medium onion, cut in wedges
1	tbsp. ginger, minced	1	cup chicken broth
3	cloves garlic, minced	1	tsp. gravy flour or cornstarch
1	tsp. seasoning salt	½	tsp. honey
1	tbsp. sherry	1	tsp. mushroom soy sauce
1	tbsp. almond oil	1	tbsp. oyster sauce
1	cup Chinese mushrooms		

Wash the chicken and cut into bite-sized pieces. Place in a bowl with the ginger, garlic, seasoning salt, sherry, and almond oil, and refrigerate overnight to marinate. Wash the mushrooms, cover with water, and leave to soak overnight. Remove and discard the stems. Slice into wedges. Heat the wok and oil. Stir-fry onions and mushrooms for 10 minutes. Brown the chicken on all sides. Add mushrooms, onions, and chicken stock with cornstarch, honey, and mushroom soy sauce. Simmer for 20 minutes until the chicken is cooked to a deep golden brown color. Serves 8.

☙

Taste is paramount. Transfer to a serving dish. Top with oyster sauce, some escallion or green onion flowers, and serve with a plate of steaming hot rice.

Chinese Steamed Omelet

½   lb. lean pork, minced

½   cup water chestnuts, minced

2   stalks escallion (green onion), minced

2   cloves garlic, minced

¼   tsp. sugar

¼   tsp. seasoning salt

2   eggs, beaten

In a bowl, mix together the minced pork, water chestnuts, escallion (green onion), garlic, sugar, and seasoning salt. Grease a medium 8-inch heatproof pie dish or steamer insert. Spread the meat in the dish and slowly pour the beaten eggs over it. Place in the steamer and cook slowly on medium-low heat for 20–30 minutes.

ભ

At home, we refer to the steamed omelet as "egg business." Make it your business to use any ground meat or fish in place of pork. Then, pair it with a cucumber salad, which is a healthy combination, but any salad will be just fine.

Corned Beef (Home-cured)

6 lbs. beef brisket

1 cup kosher salt

3 tbsp. saltpeter or Morton's Tender Quick salt

1 cup water

3 tbsp. brown sugar

3 tbsp. dried jerk seasoning

3 tsp. thyme leaves

3 cloves garlic

3 stalks escallion (green onion), chopped

1 scotch bonnet pepper, chopped (seeds removed)

3 tbsp. olive or vegetable oil

In a large mixing bowl, dissolve the salt, saltpeter, or Tender Quick in the water. Add brown sugar, dried jerk seasoning, thyme, garlic, escallion, pepper, and oil. Place and rub the brisket in the bowl of brine. Cover and place in the refrigerator, turning the meat every day, for 5–7 days. When ready to prepare, remove brisket from brine. Cook for about two hours in a pot with lots of water. Meat should be tender but not breaking apart. Cool before slicing.

೮೩

Serve with cabbage, carrots, rice, or potatoes, or make sandwiches on rye or wheat bread. Sweet pickles or coleslaw are compatible accompaniments.

Cornish Hens Broasted with Shallots

8   Cornish hens

2   tbsp. seasoning salt

12   shallots and 2 onions, peeled and chopped

¼   cup virgin olive oil

4   tbsp. ginger rice wine vinegar

4   plum tomatoes

1   tsp. thyme leaves

3   stalks escallion (green onion), chopped, and some flowers

1   scotch bonnet pepper, minced, no seeds

1   tsp. sugar, optional

Preheat oven to 500° F. In a large roasting pan, place hens on their backs. Tuck the wing tips up and behind the upper arm joint in a sort of triangle. Trust me, it stays in place. Inside each cavity, sprinkle with seasoning salt. Stuff with some chopped shallots and onion. Sprinkle seasoning salt on the outer skin, and any leftover shallots. Brush with oil. Broast for about 7 minutes, moving the hens around as necessary. Turn again after 7 minutes; the hens must be nicely browned. Check for doneness as soon as the juices run clear. Transfer hens to a platter. Skim off excess fat. Add the wine, tomatoes, thyme, escallion, pepper, and sugar. Scrape the pan, stirring until the sauce forms. Pour sauce over the hens. Decorate with green onion flowers. Serves 8.

ଔ

Broasting is my method of roasting at broiling temperature, and these little hens require about 15 minutes' cooking time. Serve with dirty rice, steamed spinach in garlic sauce, or any salad of preference.

Cow Foot and Butter Beans

1   cow foot, (5 lbs.) cleaned, cut in pieces

1   lime or lemon

1   tbsp. canola oil

2   onions, chopped

1   scotch bonnet pepper, minced, no seeds

4   cloves garlic, minced

1½ tsp. seasoning salt

3   tsp. curry powder

2   stalks escallion (green onion), chopped

2   plum tomatoes, chopped

3   sprigs thyme

1   15-oz. can of butter beans

Wash cow foot pieces in water and lime juice. Drain or dry with paper towels. In a pressure cooker, add canola oil, cow foot, one onion, pepper, garlic, seasoning salt, and curry. Stir and leave to marinate for a couple hours. Cover meat with water. Pressurize for 30 minutes. Release the pressure before opening the pot. Remove the bones and discard. Now is the time to remove any excess liquid and set aside for use later (see suggestions at the end of the recipe. Return the pot to a simmer. Add one onion, escallion, tomatoes, thyme, and butter beans. Simmer for 15 minutes. Serves 8.

ℭℨ

Cow foot stew thickens as it cools. Remember the excess liquid that was removed while cooking? This may be sweetened to taste, with sugar, Splenda or condensed milk; poured into individual ramekins, then each one sprinkled with a dash of grated nutmeg. Chill. You've now made a luscious "Cow foot jelly" dessert.

Curried Chicken

3	lbs. chicken, cut into 2-inch pieces	¼	tsp. Baronhall Farms Jamaican scotch bonnet pepper
2	tbsp. lime juice	1	tsp. seasoning salt
3	tbsp. canola oil	3	tsp. Baronhall Farms Jamaican curry powder
3	cloves garlic, finely diced	2	Irish potatoes, peeled and diced
1	medium onion, finely chopped	2	cups coconut milk
3	stalks escallion (green onion), finely chopped	4	sprigs thyme
¼	tsp. Baronhall Farms Jamaican ground ginger	1	cup water
¼	tsp. Baronhall Farms Jamaican ground allspice (pimento)		

Wash chicken with lime juice and water. Drain. Cut chicken into 2-inch pieces. Rub all over with oil, garlic, onion, escallion, ginger, allspice, pepper, seasoning salt, and curry. Allow the chicken to marinate for an hour or more. Remove seasoning and set aside to be added later. Heat the Dutch oven or skillet on medium-high heat. Add the chicken pieces and sear until light brown in color. Add a little water while searing. Add potatoes, coconut milk, thyme, with the seasoning that was set aside, and bring to a boil, uncovered. Lower the heat. Cover and simmer for 30-45 minutes, stirring occasionally, until chicken is tender and the gravy thickens. Serves 8.

လ

Serve with boiled green bananas, freshly steamed white rice and a liberal helping of Coconut Coleslaw.

Curried Goat

4	lbs. goat mutton	2	slices ginger, minced
1	tbsp. lime juice	6	grains Baronhall Farms Jamaican allspice (pimento)
2	tbsp. canola oil	3	tbsp. Baronhall Farms Jamaican curry powder
1	tbsp. seasoning salt	1	tbsp. Baronhall Farms Jamaican hot curry sauce
3	cloves garlic		
1	onion, finely diced	1	scotch bonnet pepper, minced (seeds removed)
2	stalks escallion (green onion), chopped	1	whole scotch bonnet pepper (do not puncture)

Wash the goat meat with lemon juice and water. Drain. Rub in the oil, seasoning salt, garlic, onion, escallion, ginger, pimento, curry and pepper. Cover and marinate. Heat heavy-duty skillet. Add the marinated ingredients, stirring until evenly browned. Add 4 cups water or enough to cover the meat. Cover and cook on medium-high heat. Check regularly, adding more water as needed. Cook until the meat is tender to the bone with a reduced sauce. Garnish with escallion or green onion. Before serving, remove the whole pepper and pimento grains. No one wants to bite into a whole scotch bonnet pepper. It could hurt you twice! Serves 8.

ೞ

A Jamaican get-together is incomplete without curried goat and mannish water—a very satisfying meal from a dissatisfied goat! Grandmother always said, "Tie goat eena bush, him bawl; give goat water, him won't drink; tie goat a kitchen corner, him climb the wall or mount 'pon rock-stone."

Curried Lobster

4   tbsp. canola oil

2   tbsp. butter

2   onions, chopped

3   cloves garlic, smashed, minced

3   stalks escallion (green onion), chopped

2-3 tbsp. Baronhall Farms Jamaican curry powder

1   scotch bonnet pepper, minced, no seeds

8   lobster tails, cut into chunks

1   tsp. seasoning salt to taste

1   tbsp. ginger rice vinegar

1   cup fish tea or broth

Heat skillet with oil and butter. Sauté the onions, garlic, escallion, 2 tablespoons curry powder, and pepper. Add the chunks of lobster meat, seasoning salt, ginger, vinegar and some broth. More curry powder may be added, if desired. Simmer for 10 minutes, adding more broth as needed. The sauce thickens and comes into its own, so get ready to devour. Serves 8.

❧

Lobsters have much more than juicy tails; they have meat in their claws. If patience is a virtue of yours, take your time and pick them clean. Someone will have more enjoyment.

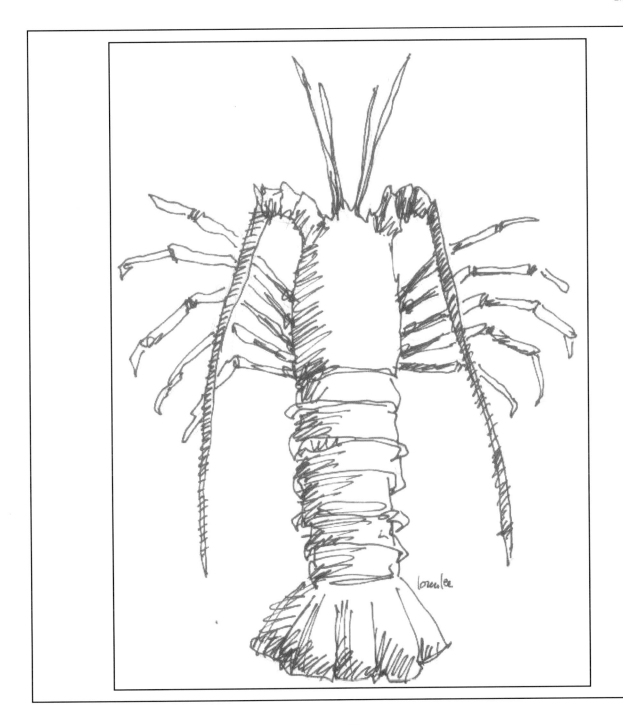

Dip 'n Fall Back (Run Down)

2	lbs. salted codfish or mackerel	2	stalks escallion (green onion), chopped
4	cups coconut milk (or 8 oz. coconut milk powder)	2	plum tomatoes, diced
1	tsp. turmeric powder	2	okras, sliced
2	cloves garlic, diced finely	1	tsp. vinegar
1	large onion, chopped	6	grains Baronhall Farms Jamaican allspice (pimento)
3	sprigs thyme	2	tbsp. fine bread crumbs (optional)
1	scotch bonnet pepper (whole)	1	red sweet pepper (cut in wedges for garnish)
¼	tsp. Baronhall Farms Jamaican scotch bonnet hot sauce		

Wash the fish and soak in water overnight to remove some of the salt, or cover the fish with water and boil for ten minutes. Drain, cool, flake fish, and set aside. In an uncovered Dutch oven, boil coconut milk until it reduces to almost custard-like gravy. Stir in the flaked fish, turmeric, garlic, onion, thyme, hot pepper, hot sauce, escallion (green onion), tomatoes, okras, vinegar, and pimento grains. Reduce heat, cover, and simmer for 10-15 minutes until the custard thickens. Remove and discard the thyme, pimento and whole pepper. If needed, add the breadcrumbs at this time. Remove from heat. Pour into a serving dish. Garnish with the red sweet pepper wedges. Serve with boiled green bananas, dumplings, or roasted breadfruit, for a real treat. Serves 8.

☙

Memories are made of this! My grandparents used our farm-grown coconuts umpteen ways. When fish was scarce, we made vegetarian "Dip 'n Fall Back," "Stop it a Pass," "Flambé Dip," or callaloo and carrots steamed in coconut milk. In the Rastafarian culture, it is called "Ital."

Flaming Red Sizzler (Beef Barbecue)

5   lbs. beef round flank steak

3   tbsp. canola oil

3   cloves garlic, finely diced

1   tsp. seasoning salt

1   tsp. mushroom soy sauce

½   tsp. scotch bonnet pepper, diced

2   tbsp. Jamaican rum

1   large onion, sliced in segments

1   red bell pepper, sliced in segments

3   stalks escallion (green onion), cut in 2-inch pieces

In a bowl, combine a tablespoon of canola oil, garlic, seasoning salt, soy sauce, and scotch bonnet pepper. Rub meat into mixture, cover, and refrigerate overnight. Prepare to barbecue the beef on medium heat (five inches away from the coals). Turn meat at halfway point. When done (20-30 minutes for medium to well-done), remove meat from grill. Prepare to sizzle just before serving: Add remaining oil to a heavy-duty serving skillet and heat on medium fire. Stir-fry the onions, pepper, and escallion (green onion) for a minute. Remove from heat and place meat in center of skillet. Pour the rum over the meat. Carefully ignite with a match and present at the table while flaming. Serves 8.

☙

When asked, what does for dinner tonight, bring on the beef for size. Set some hearts and souls on fire. Proudly announce your Flaming Red Sizzler!

Fricasseed Chicken (Cluck-Cluck)

6	lbs. whole country fowl (rooster, hen, chicken)	1	tsp. thyme leaves
1	lime (juice extracted)	2	stalks escallion (green onion), chopped
6	tbsp. canola oil	2	medium onions, diced
1	tbsp. seasoning salt	2	cups water or chicken stock
½	tsp. Baronhall Farms Jamaican scotch bonnet pepper	1	large carrot, diced
		1	chayote (cho-cho), diced
8	whole garlic cloves	2	potatoes, diced

Wash chicken with lime juice and water. Pat dry. Cut at joints, into 10 or 12 pieces. In a bowl, rub the chicken pieces with 3 tablespoons of the oil, salt, pepper, garlic, thyme, escallion (green onion) and onions. Marinate for 20–30 minutes. Separate the seasoning from the chicken and set aside. Preheat skillet with 3 tablespoons of the remaining oil. Fry chicken on both sides until brown and crispy. Add water or chicken stock, the seasonings previously set aside, and also add the diced carrots, cho-cho, and potatoes. Cook until boiling, lower the heat and simmer for 20 minutes more or until the sauce is reduced to about half the amount. Serve chicken and gravy with rice and peas, fried plantains, and a salad. Serves 8.

℆

This dish is popularly served for Sunday dinner among Jamaicans, and visitors have fallen for it too. Usually, the country fowl or home-raised hens are the best tasting—prepared this way. You have my permission to use your fingers when eating the choicest finger-licking cluck-cluck!

Fried Rice

1   lb. cooked meat, diced (beef, chicken, or shrimp)

5   eggs, scrambled

3   tbsp. canola oil

2   cloves garlic, finely chopped

6   cups cooked rice (chilled)

½   cup steamed, sliced Chinese sausage (optional)

1   cup green peas or mixed vegetables

1   cup bean sprouts

¼   cup sliced mushrooms (optional)

1   tsp. seasoning powder

4   tbsp. mushroom soy sauce

½   tsp. Baronhall Farms Hell Hot pepper sauce

¼   tsp. scotch bonnet pepper, diced (no seeds)

3   tbsp. oyster sauce

3   stalks escallion (green onion), diced

Dice cooked meat, and set aside. Scramble eggs, and set aside. Heat oil in wok. Add garlic, cooked rice (chilled rice crumbles easily with damp fingers), sausage, vegetables, and seasoning powder. Stir-fry for a few minutes. Add soy sauce, pepper, cooked meat, and scrambled eggs. Continue to stir; add oyster sauce and chopped escallion (green onion). Remove from heat. Serve while hot. Serves 8.

☙

Fried rice is my family's traditional Friday evening one-pot meal. Stir-fry all the leftover meats, rice, and veggies together in a wok. Pull your wok from the cupboard and put it to good use ... Wok your show! Within minutes, there'll be no need to ring the dinner bell; instead, your bowls and chopsticks will be clanging. Dinner is served ... no fuss or bother—easy does it! Thank the heavens that it's Friday!

Jerk Chicken

5	lbs. chicken, breasts or favorite pieces	1	tsp. thyme leaves
1	tbsp. lime or lemon juice	2	stalks escallion (green onion), chopped
2	tbsp. canola oil	1	tbsp. mushroom soy sauce
4	tsp. jerk seasoning	2	tbsp. Jamaican logwood honey
¼	tsp. Baronhall Farms Jamaican ground allspice (pimento)	4	tbsp. jerk sauce
1	tbsp. minced garlic	8	grains Baronhall Farms Jamaican whole allspice (pimento)
1	onion, diced finely		

Rub lemon juice over chicken. Brush each piece with oil and mix in the jerk seasoning, allspice, garlic, onion, thyme, and escallion (green onion). Marinate overnight in the refrigerator. Light the barbecue grill and wait until the coals are ash grey. Wipe grill with oil. Remove bits of seasonings and place chicken on the grill, skin sides up, about 6 inches away from the coals. Cover barbecue grill. Turn chicken every 10 minutes. When almost cooked, baste with a mixture of soy sauce, honey, and jerk sauce. Drop a few pimento grains in the coals to enhance the jerk flavor. Cook until meat is no longer pink. Cut meat into slices or bite-sized pieces, using a sharp cleaver and a chopping board. Serve with roasted breadfruit, rice and peas, a salad, or as a snack with hard-dough bread. Serves 8.

∞

The fire or heat may burn, the aroma will tantalize and taunt you until your first bite, and no one would ever walk away without a hearty helping of the best "jerk chick" in town.

Nyam-a-licious Stewed Peas

1   pint red peas (kidney beans)

1   lb. salt beef

1   lb. beef shank or stew

6   cups water

2   cloves garlic, diced

2   cups coconut milk

1   onion, chopped

3   stalks escallion (green onion), smashed

4   sprigs thyme

1   whole country pepper

½   tsp. Baronhall Farms Jamaican scotch bonnet pepper

½   tsp. Baronhall Farms Jamaican ground ginger

½   tsp. Baronhall Farms Jamaican ground allspice (pimento)

1   cup flour (makes 15 spinners – see Dumplings)

2   carrots, diced

Salt to taste

Wash beans thoroughly. Soak overnight in cold water. Do not drain. Wash, soak, and drain salt beef a few hours before cooking. In a large 6-to-8-quart pot, boil together the beans, salt beef, beef stew, garlic, and coconut milk until beans and meat are cooked. Add onion, escallion (green onion), thyme, pepper, ginger, pimento, and spinners. Taste before adding salt. Bring to a boil. Lower heat. Simmer for 20 minutes longer, checking consistency. If a thicker stew is desired, add a mixture of 1 tablespoon of flour with one-third cup of water. Simmer 10 minutes more. Remove escallion, thyme stems, and whole pepper before serving. Serves 8.

ఴ

"Stewed Peas," make an excellent protein dish, with or without meat. Vegetarians may add coconut milk to enhance the taste. Some like it hot, some like it cold, some enjoy it as leftovers, many days old. It is so nyam-a-licious, some are tempted to eat until "belly burst."

Oxtail with Butter Beans

2   tbsp. canola oil

4   lbs. oxtail, jointed and cleaned

6   cups water

1   tsp. seasoning salt

4   cloves garlic, minced

3   sprigs thyme

1   scotch bonnet pepper, discard seeds

2   onions, chopped

1   carrot, diced

1   cup baby lima beans

2   stalks escallion (green onion), chopped

In a pressure cooker, heat oil. Brown the oxtail on all sides. Add enough water to cover the oxtail. Add the seasoning salt, half the garlic, and thyme sprigs. Bring to a boil. Cover the pressure cooker. Set the timer to cook for 25 minutes. Remove from heat, and cool before opening the cooker. Add the remaining garlic, pepper, onions, carrot, and baby lima beans. Cook without pressure until the meat is ready to fall off the bones, and reduce the liquid to a sauce. Add the escallion (green onion). Remove from heat. Serves 8.

ɑ

Transfer the meat to a serving dish. Oxtail goes well with rice, baked plantains, and a salad.

Oyster Stew

4 dozen oysters, shucked and cleaned

2 limes, juiced

3 tbsp. butter

1 tsp. soy sauce

1 cup whipping cream

1 8-oz. cup evaporated milk

1 8-oz. cup broth

Seasoning salt and pepper to taste

1 scotch bonnet pepper, minced (seeds discarded)

1 bunch chives or escallion (green onion), sliced thinly

Clean and wash oysters to remove any grit or sand. Place oysters and butter in a saucepan. Heat until the oysters curl at the edges. Add soy sauce, whipping cream, milk, and broth to achieve a nicely colored stew. Add salt and pepper to taste. Bring to a boil, slowly reducing the sauce. Remove from heat. Garnish with chopped peppers, chives, or escallion, and serve with crackers or bread rolls.

❃

This is oyster in a stew, for those who prefer their crustaceans cooked. The aphrodisiac properties are not all lost.

Pepper Steak (Hot and Spicy)

1   lb. beef round

¼   cup soy sauce

1   tsp. sugar

1   tbsp. finely chopped garlic

½   tsp. Baronhall Farms Jamaican ground ginger

¼   tsp. Baronhall Farms Jamaican scotch bonnet pepper

¼   cup canola oil

½   cup escallion (green onions), thinly sliced

½   cup onion wedges

2   cups green and red pepper wedges

2   stalks celery, sliced slantwise

1   tbsp. gravy flour

1   cup water

Cut beef into 1/8-inch strips. Add soy sauce, sugar, garlic, ginger, scotch bonnet pepper, and a tablespoon of oil. Stir together and marinate for 15 minutes. Heat oil in wok or a deep frying pan over medium to high heat. Quickly stir-fry until meat is browned and the vegetables are tender but crunchy. Mix flour with water and add to contents in the wok. Continue stirring, allowing sauce to thicken. Serve at once with a dish of steaming white rice.

୯୫

Quick, tasty, hot and spicy … Ah-huh! Trust me, if I like it, I'm sure you'll like it too!

Polenta (Turn Cornmeal)

½ lb. salted codfish	1 cup mixed vegetables (carrots, peas, corn)
2 cups coconut milk	1 scotch bonnet pepper, minced (remove seeds)
1 lb. pumpkin, cubed	2 sprigs thyme
4 cloves garlic, minced	2 tbsp. butter
1 onion, chopped finely	4 cups water
2 stalks escallion (green onion), chopped	2 cups yellow cornmeal
2 plum tomatoes, chopped	

Soak codfish in water overnight or boil in fresh water for 10 minutes. Drain, cool, shred, and set aside. Bring coconut milk and pumpkin to a rapid boil. Add codfish, garlic, onion, escallion (green onion), tomatoes, mixed vegetables, pepper, thyme, and butter. Mix the cold water and cornmeal and add last. Bring to a boil, stirring briskly until mixture is smooth. Lower heat, cover, and steam until cooked for 20 minutes. Fluff and serve while hot. May also turn out into individually buttered ramekins or molds and serve later. Experiment with this dish. Add mushrooms or cheese to create a different flavor. Decorate with fresh escallion (green onion) flowers. Serves 8.

☙

Polenta, in Italy is a staple food. In Jamaica it is known as "turn cornmeal," served as a one-pot meal, and a similar version is fed to a man's best friend, his dog. Hence, if the action is reversed, could mean that what's good enough for the dog is good enough for man. Simply put, "try some nuh … comfort food at it's best … yeah, man!

Roast Beef (Pot Roast)

5   pounds beef round or tenderloin

2   tbsp. canola oil

2   tsp. seasoning salt

¼   tsp. scotch bonnet pepper

3   cloves garlic, finely chopped

1   tsp. garlic powder

1   large onion, chopped

1   tbsp. onion powder

1   tbsp. thyme leaves

2   stalks escallion (green onion), diced

2   tbsp. soy sauce

Mix oil salt, pepper, garlic, onion, thyme, escallion (green onion), and soy sauce together in a small bowl. Make several small, deep gashes in the meat. Stuff the seasonings into each opening. Rub remaining seasonings all over meat. Cover and marinate overnight. In a Dutch oven over medium heat, add canola oil. When hot, add a few cloves of garlic to flavor the oil, but discard as soon as they are brown. Remove the seasonings from the meat. Brown on all sides. Add a cup of water. Cover and simmer slowly. Check the pot every 15 minutes to ensure the liquid never dries out. Add water as needed until the meat is tender and the gravy is a rich brown color. To spice up the gravy, add more chopped onions, thyme, pepper, and escallion (green onion) during the last five minutes of cooking time. Cool, slice, serve, and enjoy. Serves 8.

൫

Beef pot roast is another aromatic dish, served for Sunday dinner in Jamaica. Look out! With everyone's digestive juices flowing, no one will be late for dinner. This roast will complement your rice and peas, served with gobs of gravy.

Roasted Lemon-Herb Chicken

1   4-lb. chicken, washed and dried

2   tbsp. butter

1   onion, chopped

3   cloves garlic, minced finely

2   tbsp. chopped rosemary (3 sprigs for garnish)

1   tbsp. thyme leaves (3 sprigs for garnish)

1   scotch bonnet pepper, minced (seeds removed)

1   tsp. seasoning salt

2   lemons (1 zest and juice, 1 sliced)

3   tbsp. extra-virgin olive oil

2   tbsp. canola oil

In a food processor, blend the butter, onion, garlic, rosemary, thyme, pepper, seasoning salt, lemon zest, and juice, slowly adding the olive oil to form a paste. Place chicken in a bowl. Rub the paste on the inside and outer skin. Cover and refrigerate overnight. Heat canola oil in an oven-safe skillet on medium-high fire. Brown the chicken on all sides. Preheat oven to 400° F. Transfer skillet to the oven. Roast for 45 minutes more. Chicken is done if juices run clear when pierced in the meaty thigh area. Remove from heat. Cool, carve, and garnish. Serves 4.

ℭ

Use the pan drippings, a cup of water, wine or chicken stock, a teaspoon of soy sauce, and a tablespoon of gravy flour to make the sauce. Stir to dissolve the flour. As it boils, the sauce thickens. Pour over the chicken after carving, or serve on the side.

Shepherd's Pie

1   stick butter

1   onion, minced

3   cloves garlic, minced

3   stalks escallion (green onion), chopped

1   tsp. thyme leaves

2   lbs. ground lamb or beef sirloin

2   cups water or broth

1   pkg. onion soup mix

2   cups mixed peas and carrots

4   cups mashed potatoes

¼   tsp. cayenne pepper

1   cup sharp cheddar cheese (optional)

Preheat oven to 400° F. In a skillet over medium heat, combine the butter, onions, garlic, escallion (green onion), and thyme. Add the meat. Brown while adding the broth and onion soup mix, and cook until the sauce reduces. Add peas and carrots. Transfer ingredients to a baking casserole dish. Top with mashed potatoes. Brush with butter and sprinkle with cayenne pepper and paprika. Bake for 20 minutes. For added oomph, sprinkle some grated cheese on top and broil for 2 minutes, watching closely so your casserole comes out perfectly golden. Remove from heat. Cool. Serves 8.

☙

From our English ancestors, this is a dish of merit, satisfying to man, woman, and child.

Shrimps in Thyme and Garlic Sauce

2   tbsp. canola oil

6   sprigs thyme

4   cloves garlic, minced

2   stalks scallion, chopped

¼   tsp. saffron

Salt and pepper to taste

2   cups cream

1   tsp. light soy sauce

3   tbsp. butter

2   lbs. medium shrimp, shelled and cleaned

8   stalks escallion (green onion), garnish

8   loaves French baguettes

Heat skillet with oil. Stir in the thyme, garlic, chopped scallion, saffron, salt and pepper to taste, the cream, soy sauce, and butter. When the sauce is almost reduced, add the peeled shrimps, cooking until pink. Pour the sauce over the shrimps with a spoon. Serve in individual bowls. Decorate with long escallion (green onion) flowers and a baguette on the side.

CB

Don't be afraid to dip it up. Only be aware that the sauce is so good, you may leave dem shrimps behind.

Steamed–Baked Snapper

4	lbs. whole snapper, scaled and cleaned		1	tsp. ginger wine or sherry
½	tsp. seasoning salt		3	stalks escallion (green onion)
½	tsp. garlic powder		2	sprigs thyme
½	tsp. Baronhall Farms Jamaican ground ginger		3	slices fresh ginger
¼	tsp. Baronhall Farms Jamaican scotch bonnet pepper		3	slices lemon
½	tsp. Baronhall Farms Jamaican Jerk seasoning		1	medium onion, sliced into wedges
1	tbsp. mushroom soy sauce		2	tbsp. butter

Blend together salt, garlic, ginger, pepper, jerk seasoning, soy sauce, sherry or ginger wine, and rub into the open cavities of the fish. Use a pastry brush and paint some of the liquids all over the fish. Add the escallion, thyme, ginger, lemon and onion slices. Top with dots of butter. Wrap the fish in aluminum foil and bake in a 350° F preheated oven for 15–20 minutes. Fish is done when the meat is white and flakes easily to the touch of a fork. For browning the fish, open the foil wrap; then set the oven to broil for five minutes longer, basting with its own juices. Serves 4.

❧

Decorate with escallion or green onion flowers, parsley, cilantro, or herbs of choice. Serve up a storm and have a whale of a time.

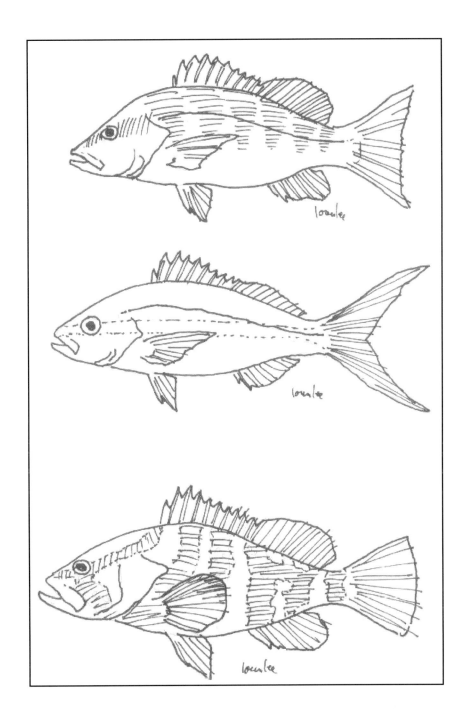

Stuffed Meatloaf Roll

2   lbs. ground sirloin

½   cup saltine cracker crumbs

2   eggs

1   cup evaporated milk

1   tsp. seasoning salt

1   tsp. thyme leaves

1   scotch bonnet pepper, minced (discard seeds)

2   onions, chopped

3   cloves garlic, minced

1   can pineapple chunks, chopped (save juice)

1   bunch cilantro, chopped

Preheat oven to 350° F. In a large bowl, mix ground sirloin, cracker crumbs, eggs, milk, seasoning salt, thyme, and pepper. Spray oil on a sheet of foil or waxed paper. Spread and press the mixture to form a 9-inch square. Add the onions, garlic, pineapple, and cilantro on top. Lift the edge of the foil or waxed paper to start rolling the meat, firmly pressing to seal the edge. Fit the roll into a lightly greased 9-by-5-inch loaf pan. Brush with half of the pineapple juice. Bake for 30 minutes. Baste again with the rest of the juice and continue baking for 15–20 minutes longer. Turn off the heat. Rest for 10 minutes. Serves 8.

☃

You're on a roll … feed your brood and they'll be rolling too.

Susumber (Gully Beans) with Saltfish

1   lb. salted codfish

3   cups susumber (gully beans)

1   large onion, chopped or diced

2   stalks escallion (green onion), chopped

2   plum tomatoes, chopped

1   tsp. thyme leaves

1   scotch bonnet pepper, discard seeds

4   tbsp. canola oil

1   tbsp. butter

Bring one quart of water to a boil. Add codfish and cook until tender enough to flake. Set aside. Cook susumber until tender. Drain. Set aside. Heat oil. Stir-fry onions, escallion (green onion), tomatoes, thyme, and pepper for a few minutes. Add flaked codfish, susumber, and butter. Stir, simmer until the sauce reduces and thickens. Transfer to a serving dish. Serves 8.

Ω

Susumber, also known as gully beans, is a bean that looks very similar to green peas, but with a slightly bitter taste, much like that of a Chinese bitter melon. Prepared this way with codfish, it is a dish to enjoy. Yes, Jamaicans serve some exotic, yet unique dishes to satisfy every taste bud. Try it with any of the following: boiled yam or bananas, roasted breadfruit, fried plantains, dumplings, or hard-dough bread and avocados, and it may also be served for breakfast any day.

Swedish Meatballs

¼	cup onions, minced		1	tsp. thyme leaves
2	cloves garlic, minced		1	scotch bonnet pepper, minced (seeds removed)
4	tbsp. butter		¼	tsp. freshly grated nutmeg
2	lbs. ground beef, round		**Sauce**	
1	cup fine breadcrumbs		1	can cream of chicken mushroom soup
1	cup half and half		1	cup light cream
2	eggs, beaten lightly		1	cup beef broth
1	tsp. seasoning salt		2	stalks escallion (green onion), chopped

Heat skillet with 2 tbsp. butter. Sauté onions and garlic until translucent and set aside. In a bowl, mix sautéed onions with meat, breadcrumbs, half and half, beaten eggs, seasoning salt, thyme, pepper, and nutmeg. Shape into 36 balls. Melt 2 tbsp. butter in a large skillet over medium heat. Brown meatballs and set aside. In the skillet, add soup, cream, broth, and stir until boiling begins. Add meatballs. Cover and simmer on low heat for 30 minutes. Remove from heat and transfer to a serving bowl. Garnish with escallion (green onion). Serves 8.

ଔ

Consider substituting low-fat milk for cream, or Alfredo sauce for soup.

Turkey Gone Chicken

1   12-lb. Butterball turkey

2   lemons or limes, juiced

4   cups pineapple and orange juice, combined

3   plum tomatoes, chopped

5   cloves garlic, minced

2   medium onions, chopped

1   scotch bonnet pepper, chopped (discard seeds)

1   red sweet pepper, chopped

1   tsp. Baronhall farms Jamaican pimento (allspice)

2   tsp. thyme leaves

2   tbsp. Lawry's seasoning salt

4   tbsp. canola oil

Garnish according to the seasonal celebration

Wash turkey with water and lemon or lime juice. Drain or pat dry with paper towels. Place in a roasting pan with juices. Blend together tomatoes, garlic, onions, peppers, allspice, thyme, seasoning salt, soy sauce, and half the oil. Rub blended mixture inside the cavity of the turkey, pushing some under the skin at the neck, down under the wings and breast. Rub some on the outer skin—using all the seasonings. Brush the remaining oil over the skin of the turkey. Cover with foil. Place in the refrigerator overnight to marinate. Preheat oven to 350° F. Roast the turkey for 15 minutes per pound. Remove the foil wrap about 30 minutes before the roasting time is up, basting regularly with juice drippings, until the turkey is a crisp, golden-brown color.

☙

Stuffing may be cooked inside the cavity of the turkey, but personally, I prefer to prepare a stuffing as a dressing, enhanced with the pan drippings. This is a turkey that will melt in your mouth like a tender piece of chicken. Having the turkey well trimmed with stuffing and things, everyone will be eager to go to town on the platter. Jamaicans or Island people in general, are happy people, quick to celebrate and let loose with food, music and playful chatter; dropping in a sly remark, like: "turkey is dressed to chicken back foot—take her down!"

Yung Nyuk (Mutton Stew)

4   lbs. goat mutton

2   tbsp. cooking oil

1   tbsp. cornstarch

1   tsp. ground ginger

¼   tsp. ground cinnamon

¼   tsp. scotch bonnet pepper

½   tsp. cumin or fennel

6   whole anise seed (Bat Guk)

¼   tsp. five-spice powder (Ng Heung Fun)

2   tbsp. soy sauce

4   cloves garlic, diced

6   lime leaves

Rub the oil over the mutton. Add the cornstarch, ginger, cinnamon, pepper, cumin, anise seed, five-spice powder, and soy sauce. Marinate for 15 minutes. Heat wok, heat oil. Drop in the garlic; add meat. Stir occasionally, while the meat browns. Add enough water to cover the meat. Cook on medium heat until meat is tender. Add lime leaves. At this point, more soy sauce may be added. Simmer for just a few more minutes, or until the stew has the right consistency and a nice brown color. Turn off the heat. Serve with steaming white rice and your choice of Chinese vegetables. Serves 8.

ೞ

This is one of my rare and ancient Oriental dishes. Many attempts have been made to find a family recipe, but to no avail. So, here it is, the way my senses of taste and smell recall. Serve up a storm!

Dip It

Have your sauce and dip it!

Cherry Butter Bing
Clarified Butter
Coffee Liqueur Butter Sauce
Dipping Sauce
Garlic Ginger Pepper Sauce
Rum Butter Sauce
Sweet and Sour Sauce
Tartar Sauce
Teriyaki Sauce

Cherry Butter Bing

1   jar Bing cherry preserves

½   lb. salted butter, softened

In a small bowl, add butter and cherry preserves. Rub together only long enough to combine, and enjoy pieces of the fruit in the mix.

ଔ

Cream cheese may be combined with some cherry preserve for a change of taste and texture.

Clarified Butter

1   lb. unsalted butter

To make clarified butter is to separate the milk solids from the clear yellow liquid. This liquid is used in baking or cooking at high temperatures, especially great for making sauces that tend to burn when regular butter is used. Melt the butter over low heat in a heavy-duty saucepan. Skim the froth and gently pour the liquid into a heatproof jar, leaving the scum behind.

Coffee Liqueur Butter Sauce

4   oz. butter

1   level cup sugar or equivalent amount of non-sugar sweetener

1   jigger Baronhall Estate Jamaican coffee liqueur

1   dash of rum

Beat the butter and sugar together until smooth. Add the coffee liqueur and a dash of rum. Mix well and serve at room temperature. Serves 8.

ೞ

"Serve you a sauce" takes on a new meaning, especially at Christmastime, when one overindulges in devouring many slices of our decadent plum pudding, oozing over with this blissful coffee liqueur butter sauce. The consequences—I'll "serve you a sauce" you'll never forget!

Dipping Sauce

¼   cup soy sauce (sang chu)

1   tbsp. honey or sugar

2   tbsp. ginger rice vinegar

¼   cup broth or water

1   tbsp. grated ginger

2   tbsp. escallion (green onion), minced

1   scotch bonnet pepper, minced (seeds optional)

2   stalks escallion, chopped

1   bunch chives, chopped

Blend together in a bowl the soy sauce, honey, sherry, broth, ginger, and pepper. Chill. Pour into a sauce dish and add escallion (green onion) or chives before serving.

ଔ

A dipping sauce serves well with any meat or seafood.

Garlic Ginger Pepper Sauce

4   tbsp. canola or peanut oil

2   cloves garlic, minced

8   thin slivers of fresh ginger

1   scotch bonnet pepper, minced, no seeds

2   tsp. soy sauce (sang chu)

2   stalks escallion (green onion), chopped

2   stalks escallion, (to make flowers)

Heat the oil in a saucepan. Cook the garlic, ginger, and pepper for a couple of minutes. Remove from heat and pour over the soy sauce and minced escallion in a heat-resistant sauce dish. Serve as a dipping sauce on the side with Bak Cjam Gai or pour a portion over the carved, boiled chicken. Serves 8.

 C3

Decorate with escallion (green onion) flowers.

Rum Butter Sauce

4   oz. butter

8   oz. icing sugar

1   jigger rum

Blend butter and sugar until creamy and fluffy. Add rum and mix thoroughly. Chill until ready to serve.

 beginsection ❧

Let personal taste determine your choice of flavor. In place of rum, try brandy, liqueurs, or cognac. Liberate yourself in the kitchen, exceed your limitations, break a few rules, and by trial and error, throw open those doors to unique and creative cooking.

Sweet and Sour Sauce

2   tbsp. honey

¼   cup pineapple juice

2   tbsp. vinegar

¼   cup tomato sauce or ketchup

2   tsp. soy sauce

1   tsp. cornstarch

¼   tsp. Baronhall Farms Jamaican Hell Hot pepper sauce

In a saucepan, blend together the honey, pineapple juice, vinegar, tomato sauce, soy sauce, cornstarch, and pepper. Bring to a boil and cook only long enough for the sauce to thicken. Remove from heat.

CB

Serve sweet-and-sour sauce with meatballs, shrimp, fish, poultry, meats, and vegetables.

Tartar Sauce

1 cup mayonnaise

2 tbsp. sweet pickle relish

1 tbsp. lemon juice

1 tsp. lemon zest

1 tsp. Dijon mustard

¼ tsp. Baronhall Farms Jamaican Hell Hot pepper sauce

2 tbsp. parsley, chopped

2 tbsp. shallots, minced

1 tbsp. tiny capers

Salt and white pepper to taste

In a bowl, combine mayonnaise, pickle relish, lemon juice, zest, mustard, and pepper sauce. Stir in parsley, shallots, capers, salt, and white pepper to taste. Chill. Serves 8.

ଔ

Tartar sauce is most popular as a dip for fish in batter, but is also a likely choice for any seafood.

Teriyaki Sauce

6   tbsp. light soy sauce

3   tbsp. ginger rice wine vinegar

2   tbsp. ginger sherry

1   tbsp. honey

2   cloves garlic, minced finely

3   stalks escallion (green onion), minced

1   finger of ginger, washed, peeled, minced

1   tsp. hot pepper, optional

In a non-reactive bowl, add soy sauce, vinegar, sherry, and honey. Add the finely minced garlic, escallion (green onion), ginger, and pepper. Rub with the back of a spoon to crush and mix the sauce thoroughly. Pour into your sauce jar for serving with fish, seafood, and meats; and, believe it or not, it goes well with vegetables, and makes an excellent barbecue sauce.

∞

This Japanese glaze has emerged, and is enjoyed by many. Oriental dishes on the whole fascinate many. You too could be creative by using some of these sauces to spice up any simple dish. And in case your wok is hiding somewhere in your pantry, pull it out, try "woking" it in your own kitchen.

Bottle It

Here are some preserves and chutneys, which are made with seasonal fruits. If prepared and stored in sterilized jars, they may be kept for up to a year. It will be a delight to pull out any of these chutneys or jellies from your pantry, and surprise your guests or family, with a topping for dessert, or an accompaniment for your meat dishes.

There is also preservation by dehydration, which is an excellent way to extend the freshness of fruits, vegetables, herbs and meats. It is a palatable way of combining dried bits of fruits, veggies, or nuts for trail mixes, snacks, treats, or as dessert enhancers, when fresh varieties are out of season. A dehydrator is fast, modern, and one of the best means used to achieve the above goals. Without a dehydrator, use the oven, with a low temperature setting of 250° F or 130ºC. Some foods need to be pre-treated with lemon juice to prevent discoloration, or by blanching to retain vitamins; some require more drying time than others. By experimenting with a variety of foods, one will soon master the art. It's a means of satisfying one's personal taste. Do not be intimidated, be creative; there's satisfaction with each achievement.

Banana Figs
Cherry Oh Baby
Cranapple Chutney
Ginger—Candied or Crystallized
Guavaholic Jelly
Guava Skins
Kumquat in Sugar
Kumquat Preserve
Mango Chutney

Mango Orange Desserve
Mango - Papaya - Persimmons - Pineapple - Plums
Orange Marmalade (Supreme)
Otaheite Apple Preserve
Pickled Mustard (Ham Choy)
Stewed Cashew Fruit
Tamarind Jam
Tamarind Preserve

Banana Figs

8   ripe bananas, skins removed

Pam canola oil spray

Spray each banana with vegetable oil. Arrange to fit on one or more tier of the dehydrator without crowding. Set the timer to 48-50 hours. After 12 hours, check if the bananas need turning over. They are done when banana are dark brown, or reduced to about one third its original size. Banana figs may be stored in jars for a week, or served pronto.

CB

In Jamaica, we have named the dehydrated banana, a "banana fig" because it has the feel and texture of the actual fruit, dried fig. However, do not be too concerned with its name, it is dehydrated ripe bananas, which is a naturally sweet treat, loaded with potassium and rich in vitamins.

Cherry Oh Baby

5   cups Bing cherries, pitted and chopped

1   lemon, juiced

4   cups Splenda or sugar

1   box Sure-Jell fruit pectin

½   tsp. butter

6   preserve jars, sterilized

Place the chopped fruit and lemon juice into a 6-quart non-reactive pot. Measure the sugar and set aside. Mix 1 cup sugar with Sure-Jell and add to the fruit. Add butter to prevent foaming. Bring mixture to a rapid boil. Stirring briskly, add remaining sugar. Return to a full boil, cooking and stirring continuously, for 1 minute. Remove pot from heat. Skim off any foam. Fill sterilized jars right away to ¼-inch from the lid. Seal. Invert jars for 5 minutes. Return to upright position. Clean with a damp cloth and set aside to cool. Store in a dry place.

છ

My name for this could be none other than "Cherry, Oh Baby." Serve over rum and raisin ice cream and listen to the remarks—almost always, you'll hear, "Oh, baby."

Cranpple Chutney

6   cups fresh cranberries, washed

3   cups Fuji apples, cored and chopped

2   cups raisins

1½ cups light brown sugar

½   cup chopped pecans or cashews

¼   cup chopped candied ginger

½   cup lemon juice

1   cup orange juice

2   tbsp. grated lemon and orange zest

3   tbsp. Baronhall Farms Jamaican Mixed Spice (cloves, cinnamon, nutmeg)

¼   tsp. salt

3   cups water

1   cup Maraschino cherry wine

In a large non-reactive pot, add cranberries, apples, raisins, sugar, nuts, ginger, lemon juice, orange juice, zest, mixed spices, salt and water. Bring to a rapid boil, stirring while still boiling for 10 minutes. Reduce heat, simmer uncovered for 20 minutes, stirring occasionally until sauce thickens. Add wine, stir, and remove from heat. Store in sterilized jars or cool and keep refrigerated. Yields about 6 x 8-oz. jars.

☙

Cranapple Chutney is a fantastically appealing condiment that whets the appetite, adding spunk to meat dishes. Deemed as a higher-notched topping, it adds essence to shortbread, scones, or sandwiches for your high tea occasions!

Ginger–Candied or Crystallized

1   lb. plump fresh ginger (washed, peeled, sliced)

2   cups water

3   cups sugar

The process for preserved, candied, or crystallized ginger comes in three stages. Place the slices of ginger in a non-reactive pot. Cover with boiling water for about an hour. Drain. Bring water and sugar to a boil. Simmer until sugar dissolves and the liquid becomes syrupy. Add the ginger and simmer uncovered until tender and the syrup thickens. Pour into sterilized jars and preserve up to 12 months. For candied ginger, remove from heat, cool, and cover and let stand overnight. Drain until the ginger is not dripping. In a dehydrator or an oven set at 120° F or the lowest setting, dry the ginger. Store in a candy jar. The syrup may be kept for making drinks or for cooking. To make crystallized ginger, drain off the excess syrup. Roll in sugar and store in jars.

Whenever fresh ginger is not available, try substituting candied or crystallized ginger.

Guavaholic Jelly

36   ripe guavas (cut into quarters)

4   quarts water

4   tbsp. lemon juice

6   cups sugar

1   pinch salt

2   small pieces ginger

Boil guavas in a non-reactive pot until soft. Cool. Strain the guavas through a jelly cloth to separate the liquid from the sediment. Guavas are loaded with their own pectin, the agent added to most fruits when making jams and jellies. Measure liquid and return to a non-reactive pot. Add lemon juice, sugar, pinch of salt, and ginger. Bring to a swift boil. Lower to medium-high heat, stirring occasionally. Continue boiling for an hour and a half or until small bubbles are visibly forming. Test if done as specified in the notes below. Remove and discard the froth or scum forming on top. Turn off heat. Pour jelly into sterilized jars. Store in a dry, non-drafty area of the kitchen and allow cooling before serving. Yield 5 jars.

☙

Know when your jelly is ready; a multitude of small bubbles overpower the pot, while stirring, the bubbles are rising. Take a test by placing a few drops in a saucer with cold water; if it forms a ball without spreading, it's time to pour into your sterilized jars.

Guava Skins

12   large Spanish guavas, peeled and sliced (save seeds)

1   tbsp. lemon juice

2   cups water

2   cups sugar

¼   tsp. almond or vanilla essence

Place the guavas in a non-reactive pan. Cover with water and lemon juice. Tie the guava seeds in a muslin bag and place in the pot. Add sugar and almond or vanilla essence. Bring to a boil. Lower heat and simmer, uncovered. The skins should be firm but tender and the liquid reduced to syrupy consistency. Remove and discard the muslin bag of seeds. Pour the guavas into sterilized jars and store up to a year. Serve with a heavy cream or ice cream.

☙

My grandmother had surprises up her sleeves all the time. She always knew when our guava trees were bare that our taste buds were itching for some well-deserved iron supplement; at the dessert table would be preserved guava skins topped with a liberal helping of homemade whipped cream—"food for the gods."

Kumquats in Sugar

2   lbs. kumquats

4   cups sugar

Wash the kumquats and slice into halves. Remove pulp, and save for later use. In a blender or food processor, add the kumquat zest and half the sugar. Grind finely. Mix in the remaining sugar. Spread evenly into a baking sheet to dry out for a few hours. Fill jars, seal tightly, and store at room temperature or refrigerate.

ಐ

These delicate little fruits are flavorful and make an unbelievable garnish for decorating cookies and cakes, an excellent sweetener for iced tea, or a zesty kumquat lemonade.

Kumquat Preserve

4   cups kumquats, sliced (pulp, seeds removed)

2   cups orange juice

3-4 cups sugar or equivalent amount of non-sugar sweetener (Splenda)

¼   tsp. grated ginger

In a heavy-duty non-reactive pot, bring kumquats, orange juice, sugar, and grated ginger to a rapid boil. Reduce heat and simmer until juice thickens, about 30 minutes. Pour into sterilized preserve jars. Seal. Turn jars upside down for five minutes. Return to the upright position. Wipe jars clean and store in a cool, dark corner of the pantry.

ക

Kumquats are miniature orange-like citrus fruits. Use kumquats, oranges, tangerines, tangelos, or lemons to make other tasty marmalades for toppings on French toast, biscuits, or scones. To make candied kumquat zest, use the same method above, leaving the zest whole or halved. Drain, cool slightly, and sprinkle with sugar.

Mango Chutney

6	firm, ripe mangoes, chopped	½	tsp. Baronhall Farms Jamaican ground allspice
1	cup tamarind puree	¼	tsp. Baronhall Farms Jamaican scotch bonnet pepper
4	tart apples, chopped		
1	cup raisins, chopped	¼	tsp. freshly grated nutmeg
1	cup orange segments	¼	tsp. ground cinnamon
½	cup pecans, chopped	½	cup water
6	cloves garlic, finely chopped	3	cups brown sugar
1	large onion, finely chopped	½	cup vinegar
1	tbsp. ginger, finely chopped	½	cup Maraschino cherry wine
¼	tsp. salt		

In a non-reactive 3-quart pot, slowly cook the mangoes, tamarind, apples, raisins, orange segments, pecans, garlic, onion, ginger, salt, allspice, pepper, nutmeg, cinnamon, water, and sugar, reserving 1-cup sugar, vinegar, and cherry wine to be added later. Stir occasionally, until the ingredients reduce to a mushy form (about one hour). Add the remaining sugar and vinegar. Continue cooking until sugar is completely dissolved and the chutney is of a rich, thick consistency. Add the cherry wine and stir to blend. Remove from heat. Cool to desired temperature. May be served right away or preserved for future use. Yields about 6 x 8-oz. jars.

ଔ

This palatable combination of tropical fruits and spices will enhance the flavor of your favorite meat dishes, and soups, or add a bit of intrigue to any sandwich ... try it for that extra "oomph!"

Mango Orange Desserve

9   firm ripe mangoes, sliced

2   cups orange supreme (segments)

1   cup orange juice

½   cup orange zest, grated

1   finger of ginger, peeled and diced

4   cups sugar or Splenda

¼   tsp. vanilla or almond extract

1   jigger Baronhall Estate Jamaican coffee liqueur

In a non-reactive pot, bring the mango, orange supreme, juice, zest, ginger, and sugar to a boil. Reduce heat to medium. Do not cover. Cook about 2 hours, stirring frequently. When the fruit and juice thickens to the consistency of butter, add the extract and liqueur. Pour into sterilized jars. Seal. Turn jars upside down for 5 minutes. This process ensures the lids are sterilized as well. Turn jars upright and cool before storing. Yields about 4 x 8-oz. jars.

ध

"Mango Orange Desserve," one of my prized concoctions, qualifies as a dessert and a preserve, hence, the name. Stores well for a year in sterilized jars, but refrigerate after opening. Serve alone as a dessert, as a filling for scones, or as a topping for ice cream.

Mango - Papaya - Persimmons - Pineapple - Plums

3   mangoes, peeled and sliced

3   papayas, peeled and sliced

3   persimmons, sliced

1   pineapple, peeled, cored, and sliced

3   plums, halved, pitted and sliced

Pam canola oil spray

Wash, peel, and remove seeds and slice fruits no more than ½ inch thick. Spray with vegetable oil and place slices of each fruit on individual trays or tiers of the dehydrator. Mangoes, papayas, and persimmons take 15–20 hours to be done. Pineapples and plums take 68–72 hours. Always check regularly; switch trays around if necessary, and ensure the fruits are well done but not overdone.

☃

Bits and pieces of fruit will be disappearing before they are cooled. Cool before storing, or keep on munching.

Orange Marmalade

8   golden ripe oranges

2   lemons

Pinch of baking soda

3   cups orange juice with segments

4   cups sugar

1   tsp. butter

Wash and sterilize six 8-oz. jars and lids in the dishwasher. Wash the oranges and lemons thoroughly. Remove the zest, leaving the white skin on the fruits. Cover the zest with water and soak overnight. Drain and cut into thin strips or chop finely in a food processor. Measure about 4 cups of zest. Set aside. "Supreme" or segment the oranges and lemons, saving about 4 cups. The seeds should be soaked in a cup of water to extract the pectin. Drain and use when boiling the fruit. In a non-reactive 8-quart pot, bring the zest with 2 cups of juice or water and a pinch of baking soda to a rapid boil for about 20 minutes. Add the pulp, cover, and simmer for about 15 minutes. Stir in the sugar gradually. Add the butter, which helps to reduce foaming. Boil for one hour, stirring from time to time, until tiny bubbles form. Take a jell-test by placing a drop in cold water, and if it does not spread out, it is ready. Pour into sterile jars. Fill jars to one-third of an inch from the top. Cover. Wipe clean. Turn the jars upside down for 5 minutes, and revert to the upright position. Cool in a draft free area. Stores for up to a year. Yields six 8-oz. jars.

☙

Incidentally, to "supreme" an orange, use a sharp paring knife. First remove the rind down to the meat of the orange. Cut between each dividing vein, slide the blade of the knife under and out to remove each segment – there you have it "orange supreme."

Otaheite Apple Preserve

10 firm apples, sliced or diced

1   lime, juiced

1   cup orange juice

1   cup water

5   cups light brown sugar

1   tsp. Baronhall Farms Jamaican ginger

½   tsp. freshly grated nutmeg

½   tsp. ground cinnamon

6   tbsp. Baronhall Estate Jamaican Coffee Liqueur

Boil apples, juices, water, sugar, allspice, ginger, nutmeg, and cinnamon in a heavy-duty stainless steel pot for approximately two hours, until fruit is tender and the liquid becomes syrupy. A few drops of the syrup in cold water will form a ball, to indicate that it is ready. Remove from heat. Stir in the coffee liqueur. Store the preserves in glass jars or cool and refrigerate for later use. Otaheite apples are seasonal, so preserve while you can. Serves 8.

CB

When Otaheite apples are out of season, invite some friends over for breakfast, brunch, or dinner. Pop out a bottle of your preserves and surprise everyone with this exotic treat.

Pickled Mustard (Ham Choy)

1   bunch mustard greens (8-10 leaves)

3   tbsp. salt

2   stalks escallion (green onion), chopped

3   cloves garlic, diced

1   hot pepper, whole

3   tbsp. sugar

1   cup vinegar

2   cups water

Wash mustard greens thoroughly to remove any sand. Drain. Cut into diagonal chunks. Place into a large bowl. Rub lightly with 2 tablespoons salt. Add escallion (green onion), garlic, pepper, sugar, and remaining salt. Pack into a preserve jar. Pour a mixture of vinegar and water into the jar. Leave to settle for a few hours. Refrigerate for at least 3 days.

Ω

Rinse and use with any favorite meat dish, chicken, pork, or salmon. Serves many!

Stewed Cashew Fruit

6   cashew fruit, sliced

2   cups water

3   cups sugar

1   tbsp. lime or lemon juice

Bring cashew, sugar, and water to a boil. Add lime or lemon juice. Stir occasionally as boiling continues. When the syrup reduces or thickens and the fruit is tender, pour into sterilized jars and store up to one year. Serve with cream or ice cream.

ᘓ

Memories are made of this—one of grandmother's specialties for us to share—enjoy.

Tamarind Jam

4   lbs. tamarind, shelled and deveined

18 cups warm water

1   lime or lemon, sliced

9   cups light brown sugar

1   tbsp. Baronhall Farms Jamaican ground ginger

8   slices fresh ginger root

1   dash Angostura bitters

Soak tamarind in water for at least two hours, preferably overnight. Knead, rub, and press through a strainer. Discard seeds and pulp. Using a heavy-duty stainless-steel pot, boil juice, lime slices, sugar, and ginger until the tamarind jells to a spreadable jam. Add the bitters. Remove from heat. Remove and discard the lime wedges. Pour the tamarind jam in Mason jars, and seal. Keeps up to one year. Serve as a topping for ice cream or on the side, for stews, curried meats, and sweet-and-sour dishes. Yields 4 or 5 jars.

ଔ

Tamarind is a mouth-watering fruit. One glance and you'll begin to drool! You may even choose to make a tamarind drink by diluting the tamarind puree with water, soda water, and your favorite sweetener.

Tamarind Preserve

8   cups shelled tamarind

8   cups sugar

8   cups water

Dash of Angostura bitters

Place the shelled tamarind in a non-reactive pot. Add sugar and water. Bring to a boil. Stir until the sugar is completely dissolved, and coats the tamarind. Add Angostura bitters. Remove from heat. Pour tamarind into sterilized jars.

ଔ

Store in a cool, dark place in the kitchen. Keeps for a year, or maybe longer.

Stressed - Desserts

How many believe desserts are stress relievers, and that there may be some truth to that theory? Classified as one of the most decadent desserts, chocolate seems to top the list for many. Not only does it relieve stress, it is chock full of aphrodisiacs—two high points right off the bat! Trust your intuition after hearing this theory. Chocolate is a derivative of the cocoa bean. Chocolate bars are made with milk, sugar, nuts, raisins, or fruits, and even though there are healthy additions, could equally be addictive. Let's play a trick by reversing "stressed" to "desserts." Desserts could be beneficial to one's health. Hence, if we agree that chocolate relieves stress, that it is a love potion capable of increasing one's libido, let the game begin—eat it, play with it, and do what you will with it.

A Browning for U (Brownie)
Baked Ripe Bananas
Beignets
Blue Drawers (Duckoono or Tie-Leaf)
Bread and Butter Custard Pudding
Bulla (John Roll)
Cassava Pone
Cherries Jubilee
Chill-out Chocolate Layer Cake
Chocolate Coffee Cheesecake
Coffee Lovers Nut-crusted Cake
Cornmeal Pudding
Crème Brulee
Cupcakes to Munch on Fudge
Easter Stout Bun for Everybunny

Flan—Egg Custard
Gizzadas
Hanky-Panky Coffee Ice Cream
Kiss My Nectarine
Matrimony
Nutty Chocomousse
Pfeffernusse Spice Cookies
Plum Pudding
Sweet Potato Pudding (Hallelujah and the Rum Punch)
Table Mango Treat
Taffy Apple Salad
Tiramisu in a Jiffy
Toto Cut-cake
Truffles

A Browning for U (Brownie)

8   oz. unsalted butter

4   oz. squares chocolate

6   eggs

2   cups sugar

2   tsp. vanilla extract

1¾ cups flour

¾   tsp. salt

2   cups pecan bits

1   cup pecan halves, garnish

Preheat oven to 325° F. Spray the baking sheet with Pam. Slowly melt butter and chocolate and set aside to cool. Beat eggs. Add sugar slowly, blending until mixture thickens. When the chocolate mixture is cool, beat with the egg, and add vanilla extract. Mix the flour, salt, and nuts, and stir into the chocolate to blend together. Pour batter into the greased pan. Stick the pecans all over the top in a decorative form. Bake for 30 minutes. Test for doneness with a toothpick. If it comes out almost clean, remove from heat. Cool. Cut into 16 pieces. Serves 8.

೫

Without much ado, here's a browning for U.

Baked Ripe Bananas

8   bananas, ripened and peeled

2   tbsp. butter or Pam spray

8   tbsp. dark brown sugar

1   tsp. cinnamon

1   tsp. grated nutmeg

1   cup orange or pineapple juice

Preheat oven to 350° F. Grease baking dish or spray with Pam. Spray bananas with oil or butter, and layer in baking dish. Mix together brown sugar, cinnamon and nutmeg and sprinkle over the bananas, covering all sides. Spray again with Pam or butter and add the orange juice. Bake for about 1 hour until the juice is syrupy and the bananas are rich brown in color. Remove from heat. Serve warm, with a dollop of whipped cream, ice cream, or chilled, creamy evaporated milk.

This is especially for you lovers who find pleasure nurturing or feeding each other—try it once and you too will proclaim that this is lover-ly.

Beignets

1½ cups water

3   tbsp. sugar

½   tsp tsp. salt

6   tbsp. unsalted butter

¼   tsp. nutmeg, grated

2   cup flour

6   eggs

2   tsp. vanilla extract

1   bottle canola oil for deep-frying

1   box confectioner's sugar

In a heavy-duty nonstick saucepan, bring the water, sugar, salt, butter, and nutmeg to a boil. Turn the fire off. Stir in the flour thoroughly. Return to a medium fire. While cooking, whip and beat until the dough forms into a ball. Turn the dough into the mixing bowl. When cool, add eggs, beating well after each addition. Add the vanilla and mix. Heat oil for deep-frying the beignets. Do a few at a time until there are 32. Cook for five minutes. Drain on paper towels. Sprinkle with confectioner's sugar and serve while hot. Serves 8.

☙

Let your hair down if you enter the New Orleans scene, because these beignets will make you out to be a glutton. After one, two, or three, you're hooked. You'll tell yourself "there's always room for one more."

Blue Drawers (Duckoono or Tie-a-leaf)

1 cup yellow cornmeal	½ tsp. Baronhall Farms Jamaican ground ginger
1 cup cassava flour or plain flour	¼ tsp. freshly grated nutmeg
2 cups grated sweet potatoes	1 tsp. Baronhall Farms Jamaican mixed spice
2 cup grated green bananas	3 cups coconut milk
1 cup grated coconut	1 tsp. vanilla extract
2 cups dark brown sugar	¼ cup raisins
½ tsp. salt	12 10-inch square cut banana leaves (quail or blanch leaves)
¼ tsp. ground cinnamon	

To "quail or blanch," dip each banana leaf in boiling water for a few minutes, to make the leaves pliable. This will allow each pudding to be wrapped, folded and tied in preparation for boiling.

Mix together in a large bowl the cornmeal, flour, sweet potatoes, green bananas, grated coconut, sugar, salt, mixed spices, cinnamon, ginger, nutmeg, mixed spice, and raisins. Place about 1/2 cup mixture in each banana leaf. (Cooking Magic bags may be used, but the color of the pudding will not be exactly like those boiled in the leaves). Fold into parcels and tie like a package, with the twine crossing in the middle. Place parcels into a large pot of boiling water and simmer for one to two hours. Slice and serve as is, or with rum butter sauce, hot or cold.

☙

In various parts of Jamaica, this sweet treat is made with cornmeal, sweet potatoes, cassava, green bananas, or may be combined. Duckoono or Tie-a-leaf got its name due to the fact that it is wrapped and tied like a parcel. The plot thickens, the name Blue Drawers is derived from the blue color and shape of a man's drawers that the pudding takes on after being wrapped, tied and boiled in the leaf.

Bread and Butter Custard Pudding

9	slices bread (hard-dough may be used)		6	eggs
6	tbsp. butter		2	jiggers (6 tbsp.) Baronhall Estate Jamaican Coffee Liqueur
½	tsp. freshly grated nutmeg		1	jigger (3 tbsp.) Jamaican rum
½	tsp. ground cinnamon		1	14 oz. can sweetened condensed milk
½	tsp. Baronhall Farms Jamaican mixed spice		1	14 oz. can evaporated milk
½	cup brown sugar		2	cups milk
½	cup raisins		2	tsp. vanilla

Preheat oven to 350° F. Grease 9 x 13 inch baking dish with canola oil and dust lightly with flour. Butter the slices of bread and cut into bite-sized cubes. Mix together nutmeg, cinnamon, mixed spice, brown sugar, and raisins. Arrange the buttered bread alternately in the baking dish with the dry mixture. Dot the top with dabs of butter. Whip eggs (do not over-beat). Add the coffee liqueur, rum, milk, and vanilla. Pour liquid mixture over the bread mixture. Allow mixture to soak for 20 minutes. Bake for 45-60 minutes or until the pudding forms a rich brown crust on top. Serve hot, warm, or cold, with or without a topping of whipped or ice cream.

CB

A down-to-earth pudding, fit to be served to royalty. The baron would attest that the taste is in the pudding.

Bulla (John Roll)

5	cups flour		1	tsp. ground cinnamon
2	tsp. baking powder		1	tsp. ground mixed spice
½	tsp. baking soda		2	cups unrefined wet sugar or dark brown sugar
½	tsp. salt		3	tbsp. melted butter
1	tsp. ground nutmeg		1	tsp. vanilla extract
3	tsp. ground ginger		1	cup milk or water

Grease baking sheets and lightly dust with flour. Preheat oven to 400° F. Sift together in a large mixing bowl the flour, baking powder, baking soda, salt, nutmeg, ginger, cinnamon, and mixed spice, making a well in the center. Dissolve sugar, butter, vanilla, and enough water to make a syrup. Pour syrup into flour mixture and bind together to form dough. Knead lightly on a floured surface. Roll out to a thickness of approximately half-inch, and use a pint-sized drinking glass to cut bullas into circles. John rolls are shaped like hot-dog rolls. Place bullas or John rolls on the baking sheets. Bake for 20 minutes. Brush bullas with water, for a crispier crust, just before removing them from the oven. Serves 8.

ଔ

I grew up watching my grandma bake the most aromatic puddings, totos, jackass corn, John rolls, and bullas in our backyard brick oven. I still recall how the sweet scents of her baked products filled the air, and often times reflect on this memorable rhyme: Bulla is a noun, big and round, soft and tender, neuter gender, take a bite and then surrender.

Cassava Pone

2 cups cassava, grated	3 cups coconut milk
1 cup coconut, grated	1 cup sweetened condensed milk
2½ cups flour, sifted	2 tsp. vanilla extract
¼ cup raisins	1 tsp. almond extract
1½ cups light brown sugar or Splenda	1 tbsp. whiskey or rum
½ tsp. salt	1 tbsp. butter
1½ tsp. mixed spice (nutmeg, ginger, and lemon zest)	

Combine the grated cassava and coconut. Mix in flour, raisins, sugar, salt and mixed spices. Stir and blend in the coconut milk, condensed milk, vanilla, almond, and whiskey or rum. Pour into a greased baking dish, dot with butter on top. Bake in a preheated oven at 350° F for about 1 hour, until nicely browned and the pudding is jelled. Serves 8.

ଔ

Cassava, also known as yucca, is used in puddings or pone and other sweet variations like cassava cake. Bammy is also made from grated cassava, wrung dry through a muslin cloth to eliminate the juice, then pressed and shaped into various round sizes. Some are made into flat wafers, and others vary from 3 to 9 inches in diameter. My grandparents, older relatives and friends would get together and tell tales they heard from their parents. The folklore and old wives tales came down the line and continue to be passed on. They spoke of "nanny," whoever was their nanny, who said eating too much cassava could cause deafness. Whether that was truth or fiction, the tale goes on to this day, and it has not hindered anyone from enjoying the cassava pone, cakes or bammies—why? Because they are so, so good!

Cherries Jubilee

4   tbsp. unsalted butter

½   cup sugar or equivalent amount of non-sugar sweetener (Splenda)

4   cups Bing cherries, pitted

1   lemon, juiced and 1 tsp. zest

½   cup cherry brandy or cognac

½   cup Baronhall Estate Jamaican Coffee Liqueur

½   gallon vanilla ice cream

In a large saucepan or skillet, over medium heat, melt butter and sugar until dissolved. Add the cherries, lemon juice, and zest, stirring gently while simmering for a few minutes until cherries are tender. Remove skillet from heat. Pour brandy into center and over the cherries. Do not stir. Carefully ignite by shaking the pan over the heat, or light with a match. Flame may be going while serving. Spoon the flaming cherries over ice cream. Serves 8.

ை

Bing cherries are seasonal, but may be cooked and preserved in jars for out-of-season use. See recipe for Cherry, Oh Baby.

Chill-out Chocolate Layer Cake

4   squares unsweetened chocolate

2   cans sweetened condensed milk

2   tbsp. Jamaica Blue Mountain coffee, brewed

2   tbsp. Jamaica High Mountain instant coffee powder

2   tsp. vanilla extract

¼   tsp. salt

1   16 oz. box graham crackers

1   16 oz. jar "Cherry Oh Baby" preserves

Combine the chocolate, condensed milk, brewed coffee, instant coffee, vanilla, and salt in the top section of a double boiler. Bring the water to a boil in the lower pot. Reduce the heat and set the top over the simmering pot. Stir until the frosting becomes creamy. Remove from heat. Cool. Meanwhile, on a flat pastry board lined with waxed paper, arrange alternate layers of 3 graham crackers, a layer of frosting, 3 graham crackers, a layer of cherry preserves. Continue that design for five or six layers. Finish the sides with frosting and the top layer with frosting and cherry topping. Keep cake chilled. Serves 8.

⋐⋑

Slice each helping with a sharp, serrated-edged knife and serve to your heart's content … Chill out, this is a no-bake cake.

Chocolate Coffee Cheesecake

2	cups chocolate wafers, crumbs	1	stick butter, softened
6	tbsp. butter, melted	1	cup confectioner's sugar
3	8-ounce tubs mascarpone cheese	6	squares unsweetened chocolate, melted
1	cup granulated sugar	1	cup whipped cream
5	eggs	1	tsp. vanilla
2	squares semisweet chocolate, melted	1	tbsp. coffee liqueur

Frosting:

Preheat oven to 300° F. In a bowl, mix chocolate wafer crumbs and melted butter. Press mixture into a deep pie dish. In a larger bowl, beat the mascarpone cheese, sugar, and eggs, until fluffy, and smoothly blended. Pour half the mixture into the crust. Stir the chocolate into the other half of the mixture, and pour with a swirling movement into the crust. Bake in preheated oven for about 45-50 minutes. Remove dish from oven and cool thoroughly. Cover and chill for a couple of hours. Choose one of the following variations for frosting. Serves 8.

 C3

Frosting Variations: Beat butter and sugar until fluffy. Add melted chocolate, whipped cream, vanilla, and coffee liqueur. Or mix 6 ounces melted semisweet chocolate, with a half a cup of sour cream and a splash of coffee liqueur. The choice is yours. After all, variety is the spice of life.

Coffee Lover's Nut-crusted Cake

2   cups brown sugar or half Splenda

2   tbsp. Jamaica High Mountain instant coffee powder

1   tsp. cinnamon powder

½   tsp. salt

2   cups flour, sifted

½   cup butter

8   ounces sour cream

1   tsp. baking soda

1   egg, beaten

1   cup pecans, chopped finely

Preheat oven at 350° F. In a mixing bowl, combine sugar, coffee, cinnamon, salt, and sifted flour. With a pastry cutter or two knives, cut in the butter to form a crumb-like mixture. Press half the crumb mixture into a greased baking dish and set aside. Stir the sour cream and baking soda together and add to the other half of the crumb mixture. Stir in the beaten egg. Scrape the mixture over the crust into the baking dish. Sprinkle with chopped pecans. Bake in preheated oven for 40 minutes. Cake is ready if it springs when touched lightly in the center.

附

Coffee lovers, you know like I do that a coffee cake is not a true coffee cake until there's coffee in it...so let's have the real McCoy.

Cornmeal Pudding

3	cups yellow cornmeal	¼	tsp. Baronhall Farms Jamaican ground ginger
1	cup flour	4	cups coconut milk
1	tsp. salt	6	cups water
4	cups light brown sugar	1	tsp. vanilla extract
½	cup golden raisins	½	tsp. rose water
1	tsp. Baronhall Farms Jamaican ground nutmeg	2	tbsp. butter or margarine
1	tsp. Baronhall Farms Jamaican mixed spice		

In a large mixing bowl, sift together flour and cornmeal. Add salt, sugar, raisins, and the dry ingredients. Stir briskly, while adding liquids. If lumps form, rub and stir to dissolve. Pour mixture into a greased Dutch oven. Dot with butter. Preheat oven at 400° F. Bake for 1½ to 2 hours. Oven temperatures vary, so check for doneness during the last half hour. Pudding must be a rich golden brown color. Remove from heat. Set aside to cool. Cooling allows the top of the pudding to gel. Serves 8.

☙

Grandma was famous for this style of baking, which may be the reason her cornmeal pudding never failed to yield such a soft, jell-like, two-inch-thick topping, that she nicknamed, "mud pon top." We used the old coal stove or brick oven method of baking, way back when, and now people are going back to their roots—rebuilding brick ovens in their back yard. Interested? Here's how we did it on the coal stove: Place the Dutch oven on hot coals, and then a tin-sheet with more hot coals as the cover. The idea is to have fire on top and fire underneath. Replenish the coals as needed throughout the baking period.

Crème Brulee

2   cups heavy cream

2   cups milk

½   vanilla bean (split)

7   egg yolks

2   eggs (whole)

½   cup sugar

4   tbsp. brown sugar

Combine heavy cream, milk, and vanilla bean. Heat to boiling or scald milk in double boiler. Remove from heat and steep with vanilla bean for 10 minutes. Scrape seeds into mixture. Using an electric mixer, combine eggs and sugar. Add a small amount of milk, slowly, to temper the eggs. Then add to the remaining milk. (Tempering the eggs is of utmost importance to avoid having scrambled custard.) Pour through a fine strainer to remove lumps and skim away foam.

Divide mixture into eight 4-ounce ramekins. Set ramekins in a large baking dish, with hot water to come halfway up the sides (hot-water bath.) Place the baking dish in a 325° F oven for 25–30 minutes until custard is set. Crème brulee will tremble slightly when done. Remove from oven. Refrigerate to chill for one hour prior to serving.

The best is yet to come. Sprinkle custards with brown sugar. Use a propane torch to quickly melt and caramelize the sugar. Or, place ramekins under a broiler for a couple minutes. Decorate with cherries. Serves 8.

ଔ

Thanks to one of my sons, Marvin, for contributing his delectable crème brulee to my collection.

Cupcakes to Munch on Fudge

2   cups flour

4   tsp. baking powder

½   tsp. salt

1 ½ cups granulated sugar

4   tbsp. cocoa (powder)

2   tbsp. Jamaica High Mountain instant coffee (powder)

½   cup milk

1   stick butter, softened

1   tbsp. vanilla extract

1½ cups pecans, chopped

1½ cups brown sugar

6   tbsp. cocoa powder

½   cup warm water

Whipped cream and berries for a topping (optional)

Prepare and grease custard cups. Set aside. Preheat oven to 350° F. In a bowl, mix flour, baking powder, salt, sugar, cocoa, and coffee. In a smaller bowl, mix the milk, butter, and vanilla. Blend with the flour mixture. Fold in the nuts. Divide batter into 12 custard cups; place on a baking sheet. Sprinkle cakes evenly with a mix of sugar, cocoa, and water. Bake for about 30 minutes. Cool. Serves 8.

ଔ

Decorate with whipped cream, fruit preserve, or fresh berries. Talk about gaining a cupcake experience, you'll eat the whole thing and feel no pain."

Easter Stout Bun for Everybunny

6   tbsp. melted butter

2   cups sugar

4   tbsp. honey

4   tbsp. corn syrup

1   tsp. vanilla extract

2   cups Dragon or Guinness stout

3   cups flour

3   tsp. baking powder

1   tsp. mixed spice

1   tsp. cinnamon

½   tsp. salt

2   cups fruits (currants, raisins, cherries, mixed peel)

2   eggs, beaten

In a saucepan, melt the butter over low heat. Stir in the sugar, honey, syrup, vanilla, and stout, until dissolved. Turn off heat. In a large bowl, mix the flour, baking powder, mixed spice, cinnamon, and salt. Add mixed fruits, liquid mixture, and beaten eggs. Pour into a greased loaf pan, 13 x 4 inches, or (two small loaf pans.) Bake at 350° F for 50 to 60 minutes—testing for doneness. Serves 8.

☛

"Have your bun and eat it." Mix it, bake it, and fill the air with the scent of spice. Sandwich some aged cheddar cheese between your buns. Happy Easter, everybunny!

Flan—Egg Custard

6   tbsp. granulated sugar

2   sticks cinnamon

2   cups water

5   eggs

1   14 oz. can evaporated milk

2   14 oz. cans sweetened condensed milk

Two loaf pans are required. Put three tablespoons of sugar and a tablespoon water in each. Preparing one pan at a time, melt sugar until caramel forms, shifting pan over heat. Remove from heat, turning pan from side to side, allowing caramel to stick to sides and bottom. Set aside to cool. Brew two cups of cinnamon tea. Set aside, and cool. In a large bowl, beat eggs. Add evaporated milk, condensed milk, and cinnamon tea. Pour equal amounts of mixture in each pan. Set pans in a larger baking pan with water (water bath) and bake at 250° F to 300° F for about 1 hour. To test if done, place toothpick in center. If it comes out clean, flan is ready to be cooled and refrigerated. Use a spatula to loosen flan from the sides of each baking pan. Flip over onto a platter, saving the caramelized syrup to serve over each slice of flan.

ଔ

"M-m-m-m-m-m-m-m...Indescribable ... Everlastingly good!"

Gizzadas

Pastry crust

1½ cups flour

½   tsp. salt

½   cup butter

¼   cup ice-cold water

Filling

2   cups coconut, grated

2   fingers of ginger, peeled, grated

1   cup sugar

½   tsp. Baronhall Farms Jamaican grated nutmeg

¼   cup water

Sift flour and salt into a bowl. Blend or cut in the butter to form a crumb-like mixture. Add ice water and toss with a fork to form dough. Shape into a ball. Wrap in plastic and chill for 30 minutes in the refrigerator. Preheat oven to 375° F. Roll out the dough on a floured surface. Cut into 12 circles. Crimp around the edge of each shell to form a half-inch ridge. Partially bake the shells on an ungreased cookie sheet. Mix together coconut, ginger, sugar, nutmeg, and water. Bring to a boil. Fill shells with coconut mixture. Bake for 20 minutes, until golden brown.

ॐ

"Gizzada," is a delish, and nutty treat, to be served as a snack or dessert.

Hanky-Panky Coffee Ice Cream

2   long-stemmed dessert compotes

6   scoops vanilla ice cream, or your choice of flavor

2   tbsp. chopped or slivered almonds

4   Baronhall Farms Jamaican roasted coffee beans

2   Maraschino cherries with stems

4   tbsp. Baronhall Estate Jamaican coffee liqueur

Sprinkle of Jamaica High Mountain instant coffee

Place 3 scoops of ice cream in each glass or compote. Top with slivered almonds, coffee beans, cherry, and warmed coffee liqueur. (Coffee lovers, here's an option for you.) Try a sprinkle of the new Jamaica High Mountain instant coffee as an additional topping. Far away and long ago, it was said, that good coffee is never made in an "instant," but this instant coffee is a wonder.

જી

Hey, you deserve to "have your hanky-panky and eat it too!"

Kiss My Nectarine

Filling:

5   apples, cored, peeled, sliced

6   nectarines, peeled, pitted, sliced

1   tbsp. lemon juice

2   tbsp. peach nectar

1   cup sugar

1   tsp. mixed spice

Topping:

1½ cups granulated sugar

¼   cup brown sugar

1   cup flour, sifted

Dash   cinnamon

1½ sticks chilled butter

Whipped cream topping

Preheat oven to 350° F. Prepare and grease an 8 x 5-inch baking dish. For the filling, combine apples, nectarines, lemon juice, peach nectar, mixed spice, and sugar. Spread mixture into the baking dish. In a dry bowl, combine the sugar, flour, and cinnamon. Use two knives to cut in the butter and the flour until a crumb-like mixture is achieved. Spread evenly over the filling. Bake in preheated oven for about 45 minutes. Remove from oven and cool before serving. Serves 8.

ଔ

Kiss my nectarine with a dollop of whipped cream!

Matrimony

6   ripe star apples (green or purple)

2   cups orange supreme (segments)

1   cup grapefruit supreme

1   14 oz. cup evaporated milk

½   14 oz. cup condensed milk

1   jigger white rum (optional)

½   tsp. freshly grated nutmeg

Remove pulp from the star apples. Discard seeds. Secure all the orange and grapefruit supreme (segments) as shown below. Combine the star apples, orange and grapefruit. Chill. Add milk, condensed milk, and white rum. Sprinkle grated nutmeg on top. Serve in stemmed glass compotes. Decorate with orange slices or sprigs of mint.

03

To "supreme" an orange, use a paring knife to remove the rind deep down to the pulp. Then, slide the blade of the knife between each dividing membrane, slicing and at the same time, gently pushing each segment out. If done carefully, there will be perfect, supreme, segments. This may be done with grapefruits as well. Nothing tried, nothing done, so give it a try and have your "supremes" to decorate many salads.

146

Nutty Chocomousse

1   cup almonds, chopped

1   cup cashew nuts, chopped

½   stick butter, softened

1   lb. semisweet chocolate, chopped

1   cup heavy cream

1   tsp. vanilla or almond extract

6   eggs

½   cup flour, sifted

½   cup sugar or Splenda

1   cup whipped cream

1   cup fresh berries

For the crust: Mix almonds, cashew, and butter, and press into the bottom and sides of a 9-inch spring-form pan. Preheat oven to 325° F. In a saucepan, over low heat, stir while melting the chocolate and cream. Remove from heat and cool for 10 minutes. Beat the vanilla and eggs gently. Now briskly but gradually beat in the flour and sugar, about 10 minutes. Fold in a portion of the egg mixture into the chocolate, then the chocolate into the remaining egg mixture. Scrape the mixture into the pan. Bake for 45 minutes, until the edge of the cake becomes puffy. Cool.

ଔ

Chill cake for at least 2 hours, preferably overnight. Serve with whipped cream and cherries or fresh fruit.

Pfeffernusse Spice Cookies

3   cups flour

1   tsp. five-spice powder

1   tsp. mixed spice

1   tsp. baking powder

¼   tsp. cayenne pepper

¼   tsp. salt

½   cup butter

½   cup brown sugar

½   cup molasses or honey

1   egg

¼   cup chopped nuts

Preheat oven to 350° F. Line cookie sheets with parchment paper. Mix the flour, five-spice powder, mixed spice, baking powder, pepper, and salt. Set aside. In a large bowl, beat the butter, sugar, honey, and egg until light and fluffy. Mix in the dry ingredients. Add the nuts. Shape into a ball. Cover. Chill until firm. Scoop, roll into balls, and place one inch apart on cookie pan. Bake for 15 minutes. Remove from heat. Cool slightly. While warm, dust with powdered sugar.

ଔ

These German Pfeffernusse cookies bring back memories of my Grandma, baking these spicy, dusted-over-with-powdered-sugar yummies at Christmastime. My treat from the boonies!

✳ *Plum Pudding*

1	lb. butter	1	tbsp. baking powder
1	lb. dark brown sugar	2	tbsp. mixed spice
2	tbsp. burnt sugar or browning	½	tsp. salt
2	tbsp. vanilla extract	1	lb. pitted prunes
1	tbsp. almond extract	2	lbs. raisins
1	tbsp. rose water	1	lb. currants
1	tbsp. lime or lemon juice	¾	lb. cherries
1	tbsp. lime or lemon zest	¼	lb. finely diced mixed peel (citron)
2	cups flour	1	dozen eggs
2	cups breadcrumbs	1	pt. each white rum, sherry, and port wine

Prepare fruits prior to baking: Wash carefully, dry, and grind prunes, raisins, and half the currants, leaving some whole to give "spunk" to the pudding. Pour enough rum and wine to cover the fruits. Soak for 4 weeks to a year in a covered jar. Cream butter and sugar until smooth. Add browning, vanilla, almond extract, rose water, lime or lemon juice, and zest. Add sifted flour, breadcrumbs, baking powder, mixed spice, and salt. Add soaked fruits, cherries, and mixed peel. Beat eggs and gently add to mixture. Pour into greased pans and steam or bake for 3 to 4 hours at 250° F. Serve with a rum butter sauce or try the Jamaican coffee liqueur butter sauce. Serves 20.

❧

An old fable says, "Eat twelve different slices of plum pudding during the twelve days of Christmas for camaraderie, health, wealth, and happiness to follow throughout the New Year."

Sweet Potato Pudding (Hallelujah and the Rum Punch)

4	cups sweet potato, grated	½	tsp. mixed spice
1	cup yellow yam or coco, grated	½	tsp. nutmeg
3	cups sugar	1	tsp. ginger, grated
½	cup flour	¼	tsp. cayenne pepper
1	tsp. baking powder	¼	tsp. salt (to taste)
¼	cup raisins	2	tsp. vanilla extract
4	cups coconut milk	2	tbsp. butter
1	jigger Jamaican white rum		

Blend together potato, yam, sugar, flour, baking powder, and raisins. Add coconut milk, rum, mixed spice, nutmeg, ginger, pepper, salt, and vanilla. Pour mixture in a greased Dutch oven. Dot the top with butter. Bake in a preheated 350° F oven for 1 hour. Pudding is softer when hot, but settles as it cools. Serves 8–12.

೫

"Hell pon top, hell under bottom, hallelujah and the rum punch in the middle!" Grandma, she was so knowledgeable, she told me that the old method of baking, with hot coals on top as well as under the pan, helps create the "hallelujah" pudding.

Table Mango Treat

4   ripe Bombay mangoes

8   scoops vanilla, strawberry, or coffee ice cream

8   tbsp. Baronhall Estate Jamaican coffee liqueur

8   Maraschino cherries

8   sprigs peppermint

Chill mangoes before serving. Cut in halves, gently twist, and remove seeds. Fill the center of each half with a scoop of ice cream. Pour a tablespoon of coffee liqueur over the ice cream; decorate with a cherry and a sprig of mint. What a treat! Serves 8.

ॐ

Bombay mangoes are best eaten with a spoon. Ideally, it is known as a table mango.

Taffy Apple Salad

1   large can pineapple chunks

2   cups small marshmallows

½   cup sugar

1   tbsp. flour

1½ tbsp. vinegar

1   egg, well-beaten

¼   tsp. ground nutmeg

1   jigger (3 tbsp.) Baronhall Estate Jamaican coffee liqueur

1   large tub whipped cream

2   cups diced apples

1   cup chopped peanuts or cashews

Day 1: Drain pineapple juice and save for use next day. Mix pineapple chunks and marshmallows. Refrigerate overnight.

Day 2: Mix juice, sugar, flour, vinegar, egg, and nutmeg. Cook until thickened. Refrigerate overnight.

Day 3: Mix coffee liqueur and whipped cream with refrigerated items. Stir in apples and chopped nuts. Chill. Serve in individual fruit compotes. Top with a twist of orange and a Maraschino cherry. Serves 8.

ଔ

Delightful is the only way to describe this "labor of love" concoction. The three-day preparation time will not dissuade your guests from asking for more; the taste conquers all.

Tiramisu in a Jiffy

2   packages lady finger cakes

3   tbsp. dark brown sugar

1   cup brewed Baronhall Farms Jamaican espresso coffee

2   jiggers of Baronhall Estate Jamaican coffee liqueur

2   jiggers rum

1   tsp. vanilla extract

4   tubs mascarpone cheese

1   cup confectioner's sugar

¾   cup bittersweet chocolate, shaved

¼   cup confectioner's sugar (for garnish)

In a bowl, dissolve the brown sugar with the espresso, coffee liqueur, and vanilla extract, to make into syrup. In a mixing bowl, beat the mascarpone cheese and sugar until soft and fluffy. Divide the mixture into three portions. Begin layering in a deep 9-inch baking dish. Place one portion of cheese, then a layer of lady finger cakes dipped in the espresso syrup, or the syrup may be poured on top of each layer. Repeat layering, ending with the mascarpone cheese. Garnish with bittersweet chocolate and confectioner's sugar. Chill. Serves 8.

❧

Replace the chocolate with cocoa powder or instant coffee mixed with confectioners' sugar. No matter how you slice it, this treat is worth its weight in gold.

Toto Cut-Cake

¼ lb. butter

1 cup sugar

2 cups flour

2 tsp. baking powder

1 tsp. Baronhall Farm Jamaican mixed spice

¼ tsp. nutmeg, grated

2 eggs, beaten

2 tsp. vanilla extract

2 cups coconut, grated

1 tsp. lemon zest

1 cup coconut milk

Preheat oven to 350° F. In a bowl, cream butter and sugar until smooth and fluffy. Sift flour, baking powder, mixed spice, and nutmeg together. Slowly incorporate dry mixture into moist mixture. Add beaten eggs, vanilla, coconut, and zest. Add enough milk and mix to a cookie-dough consistency. Transfer mixture to a greased baking pan. Bake for 35 minutes, or until golden brown. Cool. Cut into slices. Serves 8.

☙

Toto cut-cake takes the cake! Serve with a cold glass of milk.

Truffles

1   cup heavy cream

1   lb. semisweet chocolate, ¼-inch pieces

2   tbsp. unsalted butter

1   tsp. vanilla extract

2   tbsp. Baronhall Estate coffee liqueur

2   tbsp. High Mountain instant coffee powder

2   cups Pioneer cocoa powder

1   box confectioner's sugar

In a saucepan over medium heat, bring cream to a simmer. Stir in the chocolate, butter, vanilla, coffee liqueur, and coffee. Let mixture sit and cool until set. With a melon scooper, dip-up enough mixture to make small balls. Roll in cocoa powder and then in powdered sugar. Set on a platter. Chill. Yields about 36. Serves 8.

⋒

Make variations by dipping in crushed nuts or tiny bits of fruit.

Quench Your Thirst - Be Still My Spirit

Coffee heads my list of thirst-quenchers—and for valid reasons. When I was a child, I never saw my parents drinking coffee. Until I was age ten, my grandmother went shopping every Friday, leaving me with her friend, Mrs. Senior, the postmistress. She taught me a few crafts— embroidery, crocheting, and silently, with curiosity, I watched while she cooked. I still recall the aroma as she brewed her coffee on her Caledonia wood stove. The scent of coffee grew on my craftwork—lingered on my clothes; I never wanted to wash them! Little did they know about my yearning desire for just one teaspoonful, just a taste! I felt denied then, but knew with time my love would eventually lead me into the blissful world, where a well-brewed cup would fix or coffee-fy my lust for the bean and brew that still make me go nuts! I'm especially nuts about my native country's coffees—the world famous and the Rolls Royce of coffees—Jamaica Blue Mountain coffee. Falling almost on par—a taste you could get hooked on—Baronhall Estate Jamaican gourmet coffee; talk about nuts—you'll go nuts and never know what hit you—one cup and you'll never look back.

Coffee, a thirst-quencher, may be served hot or cold. Modern inventions and multinational concoctions have created choice roasts, decaffeinating, and added flavors. The French roasts or espresso roasts are the rage for espressos, cappuccinos, lattes, and iced coffee drinks. Believe this or not—Coffee is a most invaluable aphrodisiac—use it when needed to stay awake for those marathon workouts with your significant other; even for those tête-à-tête moments—it lifts the libido sky-high—prolongs the sex drive—no respecter of gender. Coffee - anyone?

Here, let me share some techniques and practical tips to help preserve or prolong the shelf life of your beans, yielding a perfect brew every time:

~Gadget guru suggests that a French press is a must-have; splurge on a multi-purpose coffee percolator-cappuccino machine-grinder-timer, all the perks in one machine. At the touch of a button, coffee poureth over.

~Purchase only freshly roasted beans instead of ground coffee.

~Beans can be stored safely in the freezer up to three months.

~Grind only enough beans for each brew. Measure two tablespoons beans or one heaping tablespoon ground coffee per cup of water.

~Use ice-cold purified or distilled water for a tastier brew.

~A pinch or a dash of salt heightens the taste of coffee.

~Consume freshly brewed coffee within 20 minutes or flavor and crispness diminishes.

~Remove ground coffee from the machine as soon as the brewing cycle ends.

~Freeze leftover brew for use as coffee cubes in iced coffee drinks.

~Here's my brawta or tip for gardeners: Toss used coffee into the garden to help deter intruding pets, like cats, or pests, like ants. While enhancing the blooms of your flower garden, feel secure, knowing you have a user-friendly pesticide or fertilizer.

Coffee	Lime or lemonade
Country Chocolate Tea	Lime Squash
Egg Flip	Otaheite Apple Drink
Fruit Punch	Sorrel
Ginger Beer	Soursop Nectar
Iced Tea	Tamarind Fizzy
June Plum Drink	

Country Chocolate Tea

8   1-inch balls country chocolate

2   cinnamon sticks or 6 leaves

10 cups water

½   tsp. salt (to taste)

½   tsp. freshly grated nutmeg

1   cup coconut milk (optional)

1   cup sweetened condensed milk

Boil chocolate and cinnamon in water, using a non-reactive pot, uncovered. Add salt to taste. Stir in nutmeg and coconut milk. Bring to a boil. Lower heat and simmer for 10 minutes. Strain. Sweeten to taste. Serves 8.

ᘓ

Taste the knockout, down-to-earth goodness of country chocolate. To Jamaicans, "tea" is relative, as in something we drink at breakfast or high tea. "All-a-tea—a-same-tea!"

Egg Flip

3   egg yolks

2   tbsp. sugar or equivalent amount of non-sugar sweetener

1   cup milk

1   cup cream

2   tbsp. sweetened condensed milk

½   tsp. vanilla or almond extract

½   tsp. grated nutmeg

2   cinnamon sticks

2   cups Jamaica Blue Mountain or Baronhall Estate Jamaican coffee, brewed

Beat eggs and sweetener until fluffy and evenly yellow in color. Heat milk—do not boil. Whisk briskly into eggs—the milk, condensed milk, vanilla, or almond extract. Sprinkle some nutmeg on top. Serve hot with a cinnamon stick stirrer, or over crushed ice for a cold flip.

ଓ

Add a shred of lemon zest for an alternative twist, or a cup of hot coffee to lift it a perk higher!

Fruit Punch

4   cups orange juice

4   cups pineapple juice

2   lemons or limes, juiced

2   cups cherry or strawberry Jell-O (dissolved, cooled, not jelled)

1   cup green tea

1   packet cherry Kool-Aid, dissolved in 4 cups water

1   cup strawberry syrup

1   cup sugar or equivalent amount of Splenda

2   cups sparkling soda (lemon-lime)

Angostura bitters

2   cups frozen fruit cocktail

In a 6-quart punch bowl, blend together orange, pineapple, and lemon juices, Jell-O, tea, Kool-Aid, syrup, and sugar. Chill. Serve with club soda, a dash of bitters, and frozen fruit.

☙

Go – punch – go! Punch me over and pour me out!

Ginger Beer

4   quarts water

1   lb. ginger root

½   cup lime or lemon juice

½   cup rice

8   grains pimento (allspice)

6   cups sugar

Bring water to a rapid boil in a stainless steel pot. Peel and grate or chop ginger. Add the ginger, lime or lemon juice, rice, and pimento grains to the water. Turn off heat, cover the pot, and steep for 3 or 4 days. Strain, sweeten, and pour into serving decanters. Chill. Serve with cracked ice. Rum may be added, if desired. Serves 20.

 beta

Here's to one "hot to trot" drink!

Iced Tea

8   cups tea (English, Earl Grey, or Chinese green tea)

¼   cup lemon juice

8   sprigs mint

8   cinnamon sticks

8   lemon slices and lemon zest

Begin by brewing one teaspoon of loose tea per cup of very hot, not boiling water, steeping for 5–10 minutes. Strain. Sweeten to taste. Refrigerate to chill. At time of serving, pour over crushed ice. Add some personal touches—decorate with mint sprigs, lemon slices, or a sliver of zest, then a cinnamon stick for stirring pleasure and flavor.

೦೩

For those who enjoy herbal teas, try some of these:

Basil relieves headaches, indigestion, and calms the nerves.
Chamomile soothes the nerves to reduce insomnia.
Cerasee is good for colds and stomach cleansing.
Dandelion relieves bladder problems.
Ginger for colds, nausea, and stomach gases.
Lemongrass is great for fevers and upset stomach.
Lime leaves for headaches and upset stomach.
Peppermint for indigestion and nausea.
Spanish needle for colds and indigestion.
Susumber leaves for colds.
Thyme for chest congestion and kidney stones.
Vervain or verbena for calming the nerves and stomach flu.

Always consult with your personal physician before taking herbal remedies.

June Plum Drink

12 June plums

2 fingers ginger, peeled and diced

8 cups of water

2 limes, juiced

1 cup sugar or equivalent amount of non-sugar sweetener

Slice away the meat of the plums and discard the thorny seed. Puree the June plum, ginger, water, and lime juice in a blender. Strain. Sweeten to taste. Chill or serve over crushed ice. Decorate with lime wedges or zest.

ෆ

This is a seasonal fruit, like many of the tropical fruits, so freeze some fruit or juice for out-of-season delightful treats.

Lime or Lemonade

5   lemons or 10 limes

8   cups water

1   cup sugar or equivalent amount of non-sugar sweetener

½   cup strawberry syrup for pink lemonade

Pour water in a 2-quart pitcher. Add lemon or lime juice (use half of each for a variation). Sweeten to taste. Again, do your thing with any combination of sweeteners (sugar, non-sugar, or syrup). Dress each glass with a slice or a twist of lemon. Serves 8.

೮೫

In my neck of the woods, we produced lots of citrus—lemons, limes, Seville (bittersweet) oranges, grapefruits, navel oranges, tangerines, and ortaniques. It was our privilege to manufacture and enjoy umpteen varieties of preserves, juices, and drinks.

Lime Squash

4   cups soda water

2   limes, juiced and 1 cut in 4 wedges

4   tbsp. strawberry syrup

4   cherries with stems

Pour soda water, lime juice, and syrup into a pitcher with crushed ice. Stir. Pour into individual highball glasses and decorate with a cherry, a wedge of lime or lemon, and a straw or stirrer—deliver with a smile.

ꞔꞗ

If you are out of limes, but blessed with lemons or kumquats, these two sexy alternatives may convince even the fellows to try your kumquat-lemon squash and have a mellow bash!

Otaheite Apple Drink

2   dozen Otaheite apples

2   quarts water

2   slices fresh ginger

2   tbsp. lemon or lime juice

2   cups sugar or equivalent amount of Splenda (non-sugar sweetener)

Remove seeds from the apples, cut into slices, and place in a blender with the water, ginger, and lemon juice. Divide into two batches. Pulse or liquefy each batch for a few minutes. Strain. Sweeten to taste. Store in refrigerator until chilled or serve immediately over crushed ice. Adorn each glass with a sliver of apple, a cherry, or a sprig of mint. Serves 8.

 C3

Some make this drink by boiling the fruit—try my method—totally enjoy the "fresh squeeze!"

Sorrel

3   quarts boiling water

8   cups fresh sorrel sepals or 2 cups dried sorrel

½   lb. ginger root, crushed or chopped finely

12   grains allspice (pimento) or 6 cloves

2   tbsp. rice, uncooked

3   cups sugar or equivalent amount of Splenda (non-sugar sweetener)

In a large non-reactive pot, bring water to a boil. Add sorrel, ginger, pimento and rice. Return to a full boil. Turn off heat. Cover. Steep for 3 days. Strain, sweeten, and chill. Serve in cocktail glasses or brandy snifters. Add crushed ice, rum, or wine, if desired. Serves 12.

At Christmas, sorrel is served at every Jamaican table. It is known to be rich in vitamins, minerals, and powerful antioxidants—helpful in warding off diseases. Could this be a liquid pill? Invited to friends' for dinner? Take a bottle of this rich red brew—makes a welcome gift.

Soursop Nectar

1   soursop, ripened (see Aphrodisiacs and Other Foods)

6   cups water

1   cup sweetened condensed milk

2   limes or lemons, juiced

1   cup sugar or equivalent amount of Splenda

¼   tsp. grated nutmeg

Wash soursop. Remove and discard the skin and seeds. Place the pulp and water in a blender. Puree. Extract the nectar by pouring through a sieve or strainer. Sweeten with condensed milk for a creamy consistency. Optionally, create a lighter drink by adding lime or lemon juice. Sweeten with sugar or Splenda. Chill. Serve with a dash of nutmeg to add a bit of oomph! Serves 8.

૭૩

There is a belief that this nectar is exceptionally good for strengthening and soothing the nerves! Soursop ice cream is made using this nectar.

Tamarind Fizzy

2   cups tamarind, shelled

2   fingers ginger, diced

1   lime or lemon, juiced

6   grains Baronhall Farms Jamaican pimento (allspice)

8   cups water

2   cups sugar or equivalent amount of Splenda

½   tsp. baking soda (optional)

4   cups sparkling soda

8   lemon wedges

In a non-reactive bowl, soak the tamarind, ginger, lime juice, and allspice in the water for about 8 to 12 hours. Rub with a wooden spoon to remove the pulp from the seeds. Strain and sweeten to taste. Chill. Prior to serving, add baking soda or sparkling soda to create this fizzy drink. Serve over crushed ice with a wedge of lemon. Serves 8.

ognál

You have the option of substituting sparkling soda water for baking soda.

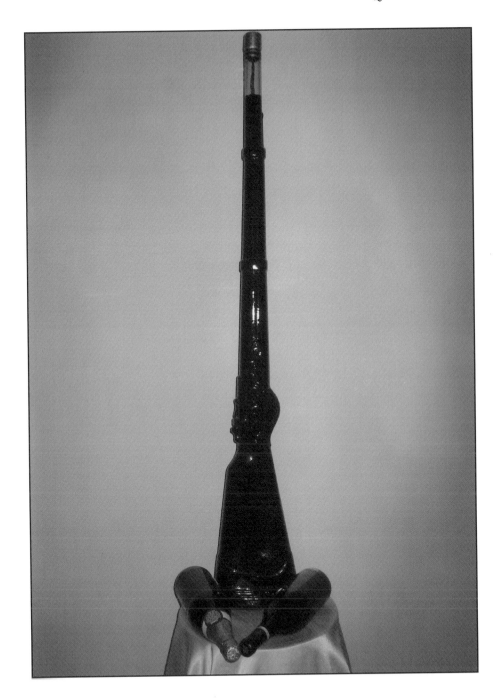

Whet Your Lips—Shots From The Bar

Take a bow to some after-dinner drinks in this segment. Savour every sip as it hits the taste buds or palate—gulp and you gulp alone! Remember, a timely glass of liqueur, cognac, dessert wine, or brandy of choice, could bring pure pleasure and sensuality (a second glass is in order).

Here are a few tips for wine lovers. If a wine cellar is not on your priority list, keep your wines in a cool, dark cupboard. A steady temperature control of 65° F is quite suitable, and more favorable than one that fluctuates between 45° F to 75° F. I like to stock up on a few reds, a couple of whites, and my most favorite, some vintage ports. They will do fine under these conditions. A bit of humidity is also helpful, if only to keep that cork moist, which is the reason why wines are stored lying down. If for any reason the wine leaks, check the corks, and use that wine for cooking.

Caution—consuming too many of these tongue-twister shots may cause drowsiness, impair vision, impede driving ability—rendering one to frunk to duck.

1-2-3—Easy Does It
Café "Casanova"
Coffee au Liqueur
Coffee Brandy Alexander
Coffee Cognac Mint on Mint
Eggnog
Guinep Liqueur
Orange Liqueur
Rattlesnake in the Glass
Rum Punch Panty Dropper

1-2-3–Easy Does It

1   jigger of gin or vodka

2   jiggers of grape juice

3   jiggers of ginger beer

Measure: 1 jigger equals 3 tablespoons

Mix a jigger of gin or vodka with two jiggers of grape juice and three jiggers of ginger beer. Serve over crushed ice and garnish with a sprig of mint.

ᜥ

Vodka may be a good substitute for gin…

But think it over—perhaps you wish not to sin …

Caution! I know not—which is the better evil …

Remember the story of the boll weevil …

He could eat all your goods in a day …

Vodka could equally have its own way …

Oh heck! Bite the d … bullet …

After 1-2-3 — Easy does it! …

Cafe "Casanova"

2   4- or 6-ounce cappuccino mugs (thick, heatproof)

4   tbsp. Baronhall Estate Jamaican coffee liqueur

2   tbsp. Jamaican gold rum

2   tbsp. granulated sugar

1   tsp. ground cinnamon

2   cups brewed Baronhall Estate Jamaican coffee

4   tbsp. whipped cream

1   tsp. Jamaica High Mountain instant coffee

Wet the rim of each mug with coffee liqueur. Dip in sugar and cinnamon to coat the edge. In a small pot, warm the rum and coffee liqueur. Pour the warmed mixture into each mug and swish around to coat the inside. Ignite with a match—rotate mug lightly to melt sugar. Add freshly brewed coffee, whipped cream, and a sprinkle of instant coffee. Serves 2.

CЗ

Lovers of coffee everywhere—on romantic, playing with your brew evenings—whipped cream adds pleasure—you may be playing with fire—no need to get burned—have your "Panther" on hand. Here's to you, Casanova!

Coffee au Liqueur

1   cup brewed coffee, chilled

6   tbsp. milk or cream

2   jiggers (6 tbsp.) Baronhall Estate Jamaican coffee liqueur

2   tbsp. whipped cream

1   tsp. instant coffee or cinnamon

3   roasted coffee beans

Layer in two shot glasses or glass coffee mugs, the coffee and cream. Add a shot or two of the coffee liqueur. Top with whipped cream, a dusting of instant coffee, cinnamon, or three coffee beans. Serves 2.

ఴ

Hear ye, this country bar chatter about liquor …

The pronunciation for liquor is lick-her!

Rum, Rum, Rum "sweet can't done!"

Brandy will make Sandy dandy all the time!

Gin will definitely make you sin!

And surely, whiskey will make you very frisky!

Coffee Brandy Alexander

1 cup evaporated milk

½ cup Baronhall Estate Jamaican coffee liqueur

½ cup brandy

12 coffee cubes (frozen leftover coffee)

Pour the milk, liqueur, brandy, and iced coffee cubes into a blender or a shaker. Strain into chilled cocktail glasses. Top with stemmed cherries, sprigs of mint, or a dollop of ice cream. Serves 8.

ଔ

Bottoms up!

Coffee Cognac Mint on Mint

1   jigger Baronhall coffee liqueur

1   jigger cognac

1   jigger white crème de menthe

1   jigger cream

4   iced coffee cubes

1   sprig peppermint leaves

Measure: One jigger equals three tbsp.

Pour the liqueur, cognac, and crème de menthe together into a shaker with iced coffee cubes. Shake, strain, and serve in a cocktail glass. Top with a sprig of mint leaves.

છ

Softly and smoothly, it caresses the tongue—wending its way down the hatch!

Eggnog

6   eggs

½   cup sugar or equivalent amount of non-sugar sweetener

¼   tsp. salt

4   cups cream

1   cup sweetened condensed milk

1   cup each brandy and Baronhall coffee liqueur

3   tsp. vanilla extract

1   tsp. grated nutmeg

Beat eggs until fluffy. Stir sugar and salt with cream and milk. Heat, but do not boil. Gently and slowly whisk the warm milk into eggs. Add brandy, liqueur, vanilla, and nutmeg. Serve chilled. Serves 8.

℘

Eggnog or Egg Flip—if you cannot decide which to have, do both or flip a coin. Tails, go non-alcoholic; heads, go for the alcoholicious!

Guinep Liqueur

8   cups guineps (pluck the fruit from the outer shell)

1   finger ginger, peeled and chopped

1   cup lemon juice

2   tbsp. lemon zest

4   cups brown sugar

1   bottle vodka

1   pint or flask of Jamaican white rum

1   large glass jar

Place plucked guineps in a non-reactive pot with ginger, lemon juice, zest, and sugar. Heat only to boiling point, stirring to dissolve the sugar. Cool. Add vodka and rum. Cover and leave to rest for one week. Pass through a fine strainer. Pour in sterile liqueur bottles.

&#x03;

Guineps are a pulp-like fruit, very similar to lychees, and are plentiful in Jamaica during the summertime. A taste of guinep liqueur and your spirit soars to heights unknown … a tonic that spits iron.

Orange Liqueur

6   oranges

3   cinnamon sticks

6   cloves

12 grains allspice

1½ cups sugar

6   cups vodka

2   lemons, zest

1   wide-mouthed jar

Wash oranges. Use a sharp knife or fork to punch holes all around the fruit. Place in a wide-mouthed jar. Add cinnamon sticks, cloves, allspice, and sugar. Pour one or two bottles of vodka, enough to cover the fruit. Steep for 5 days. Add lemon zest on the third day. Strain and pour into sterile liqueur bottles. Store in a hidden section of the pantry cupboard, away from bright lights.

&

Homemade liqueurs are at their best after resting for a month. Serve at room temperature.

Rattlesnake in the Glass

2 tbsp. Baronhall Estate Jamaican coffee liqueur

2 tbsp. cognac

2 tbsp. Bailey's Irish cream

Layering shots like these, require gentle, careful, steady hands. First, pour the Baronhall Estate Jamaican coffee liqueur in a tall shot glass. Place a bar spoon in the glass, back side up; slowly pour the cognac as a second layer. Repeat, still using the bar spoon, and gently pour the Bailey's Irish cream as the top layer. Serve gingerly.

ଔ

When there's a rattlesnake in your glass, never ask what size it is; one of those times when size does not matter; go bottoms up!

Rum Punch Panty Dropper

1 cup lime or lemon juice

1 cup granulated sugar

½ cup strawberry syrup

½ cup honey

2½ cups Jamaican white rum

½ cup Baronhall Estate Jamaican coffee liqueur

4 cups cold water

½ tsp. Angostura bitters

Garnish: 2 cups pineapple chunks and frozen pineapple juice cubes.

In a large bowl, combine lime or lemon juice, sugar, syrup, honey, white rum, coffee liqueur, water, and bitters. Stir thoroughly to dissolve sugar. For a mellow blend, aging is necessary. Allow mixture to stand in a cool place for a few hours prior to serving. Serve in punch glasses garnished with bits of fruit, frozen cubes of pineapple juice, or crushed ice. The basic guideline for making rum punch is: one part sour (lime juice), two parts sweet (sugar, syrup, honey), three parts strong (rum), four parts weak (water, juice, crushed ice) and a dash of Angostura bitters.

☙

Don't worry! Drink and be merry! Have a super party! Interpret the title as your taste allows!

Brawta

Brawta is a word used in Jamaican lingo, which defines the act of bartering for more at the end of a deal or shopping experience—asking for extras, or giving a bonus, or a tip. Here's my "brawta" to you:

Baked Ripe Plantains
Callaloo and Saltfish
Dirty Rice with Ground Round
Dumplings
Fruit Salad
Gnocchi Galore
Hoppin' John (Rice and Black-eyed Peas)
Jackass Corn
Macaroni and Cheese
Roasting Breadfruit
Scalloped Potatoes
Seasoned Rice
Stuffed Turkey Dressing

Baked Ripe Plantains

4   ripe plantains

2   tbsp. clarified butter

2   tsp. cinnamon

1   tsp. nutmeg, grated

4   tbsp. brown sugar

Preheat oven to 350° F. Lightly spray baking dish with Pam. Peel and slice each plantain into four diagonal pieces, two inches in length. Brush with clarified butter or spray with Pam. Make a mixture of cinnamon, nutmeg, and brown sugar. Sprinkle all over the plantains. Bake for about 45 minutes, turning halfway through. Remove from oven when done to a rich brown color. Serves 8.

ଔ

Try this for variety: Cut off both ends of a half-ripened, turn or green plantain. Split the skin lengthwise. Bake in the skin for 15 minutes in a microwave oven. Remove from oven. Use a rolling pin to flatten the plantain, while it is still in the skin. Peel. Slice into three-inch pieces. Brown the pieces on both sides, in a heated skillet, with oil or clarified butter. Sprinkle with salt. Serve as a side dish or as a snack. Delish!

Callaloo and Saltfish

1   lb. codfish

1   bunch callaloo, washed, stripped

2   tbsp. canola oil

2   tbsp. butter

4   cloves garlic, minced

2   onions, wedges

3   stalks escallion (green onion), diced

Seasoning salt to taste

1   scotch bonnet pepper, minced, without seeds

2   plum tomatoes, chopped

2   sprigs thyme

Place the codfish to soak overnight in a bowl of water. Drain, and remove bones, flake, and set aside. Wash, strip, and cut up the callaloo into 2-inch pieces, or smaller. In a heated saucepan, add half the canola oil, and half the butter. Sauté half the garlic and onions; add the callaloo with salt to taste. Cover and allow it to steam in its own juice for five minutes. Remove from heat. Drain. Transfer to a serving dish. In a skillet, heat the other half of the oil and butter. Sauté the garlic, onion wedges, escallion (green onion), scotch bonnet pepper, tomatoes, and thyme. Add the flaked codfish. Simmer uncovered, stirring a couple times. When the liquid reduces, transfer the fish to the callaloo dish. To stir or not to stir, this is a delicious combination. Serves 8.

ℭ

Callaloo and saltfish may be served with yellow yam, roasted breadfruit, or fried plantains. Partake of it for breakfast, lunch or dinner. Use the leftovers, if any, to make some delightful sandwiches; step it up another notch by adding some rice, coconut milk, and pumpkin, and in 20 minutes, you made yourself some seasoned rice; another meal, just like that.

Dirty Rice with Ground Round

2   tbsp. canola oil

2   cloves garlic, minced

1   onion, chopped

1   lb. ground round of beef

1   tsp. seasoning salt

4   cups broth or boiling water

2   cups rice

2   stalks escallion (green onion), chopped

1   red sweet pepper, seeded and diced

2   stalks celery, peeled and diced

1   scotch bonnet pepper, seeds removed

1   tsp. thyme leaves

1   tbsp. oregano leaves

2   tbsp. finely chopped cilantro

2   tbsp. butter

In a skillet, heat oil. Add garlic, onions, ground beef, and seasoning salt. Cook until meat is browned. Add broth, rice, escallion (green onion), sweet pepper, celery, pepper, thyme, oregano, cilantro, and butter. Bring to a boil. Lower the heat, cover and simmer for 25 minutes. Serves 8.

೮೩

Fluff the dirty rice with a fork. Serve with any meat dish or salad. Dessert is up in the air!

Dumplings and Spinners

4   cups flour

1¼ cups water

Salt to taste

Mix the flour, water and salt together, kneading until the dough is stiff. Break into pieces. Roll each piece into a ball, flatten and shape into a wheel-like circle, or form into shapes of your choice. Cook dumplings in boiling salted water for 20 minutes. Dumplings are a great addition to soups and stews. Serve as a carbohydrate with any main dish, like ackee and salt fish or mackerel rundown. Serves 8.

ରେ

Dumplings vary in sizes, shapes, and kinds. Small, squiggly shapes are "spinners," those rolled into a barrel shape are "pot bellies," and the great big round ones are nicknamed "cartwheels," mainly cooked by farmers in the fields. For other variations, try cassava or cornmeal dumplings. Use one cup of cornmeal or cassava to two cups of flour.

Fruit Salad

1   Fuji or red delicious apple, diced

4   bananas, sliced or diced

2   orange, supreme segments

1   grapefruit, supreme segments

1   mango, peeled and diced

40 grapes

Strawberry syrup or condensed milk

Freshly grated nutmeg, optional

In a bowl, combine fruits in the order suggested. Use the juice of the oranges and grapefruit to cover the apples or bananas; this will prevent oxidation and keep the fruits from darkening. Cover and chill. If desired, fruit salad may be served alone, or sweetened to taste with syrup or condensed milk. A dash of grated nutmeg is optional.

♋

My basics for a fruit salad are oranges, bananas, mangoes, and apples. Select seasonally available fruits to satisfy your taste.

Gnocchi Galore

2   lbs. potatoes

1   tsp. salt

2   eggs, well beaten

2   cups flour

Wash and cook the potatoes until tender. Cool, peel, and mash. In a bowl, combine potatoes, salt, and eggs. Knead with the hands, adding just enough flour to form dough. On a floured surface, roll out pieces of the dough. Shape into ropes with both hands. With a sharp knife, cut crosswise into one-inch lengths. These may also be rolled by hand to form dumplings of any shape. Bring a pot of salted water to a boil. Add gnocchi. Cook for 3 minutes until they float. Scoop them out with a colander, drain, and arrange in a serving bowl. Add butter or sprinkle some cheese on top. They may also be served like noodles, with meat sauce.

☙

Somewhere in my youth, these plain old potato dumplings were made with sweet potatoes. The highfalutin name gnocchi is Italian. Gnocchi are really knuckle-sized potato dumplings for the child in all of us. Let's do it and enjoy some oldies but goodies.

Hoppin' John (Rice and Black-eyed Peas)

1	pint dried black-eyed peas
4	ounces salt beef brisket
2	cups coconut milk
4	stalks escallion (green onion), chopped
2	cloves garlic
4	sprigs thyme
½	tsp. Baronhall Farms Jamaican scotch bonnet pepper
6	grains Baronhall Farms Jamaican whole allspice (pimento)
1	whole green scotch bonnet pepper
4	cups rice

Soak peas in 8 cups of water overnight. Soak salt beef separately in water overnight. Place peas and water, drained salt beef, coconut milk, escallion (green onion), garlic, thyme and pepper in a heavy-duty six-quart pot. Cook gently for approximately 1½ to 2 hours until peas are tender but not mushy. Add rice, whole scotch bonnet pepper, and enough water to bring water level 3/4 inch above peas. Add salt if desired. Bring everything to a boil. Cover and simmer for 15 to 20 minutes longer, shifting pot around every few minutes. Turn off heat and allow it to sit for 10 minutes before stirring. Rice should be of a grainy texture. Before serving, remove thyme, pimento grains, and pepper. Serve alone or with your favorite meat dish. Serves 8.

෧

"Hoppin' John" is an American Southern dish of rice and black-eyed peas, traditionally served on New Year's Day to bring good luck all year. Superstitiously, the black-eyed peas are compared to a dark-eyed man. If one comes dancing as your first visitor on New Year's Day, good luck follows all year. Similarly, Jamaicans are of like mind in their beliefs and superstitions. A celebration would not be without rice and black-eyed peas for Christmas and New Year's dinners.

Jackass Corn

3   cups flour

1   tsp. baking powder

½   tsp. mixed spice

¼   tsp. salt, optional

1   coconut, grated

2   tsp. ginger, grated

2   tbsp. butter

1½ cups light brown sugar

1   cup water

Preheat oven to 375° F.   Sift together the flour, baking powder, mixed spice, and salt.   Add the coconut, grated ginger, butter, sugar, and a little water, while mixing to form the dough.   Flour the pastry board and rolling pin. Roll out the dough thinly.   With a cookie cutter, cut into 24 rounds, squares, or any desired shape.   Bake on an ungreased cookie sheet for about 25 minutes. They should be crispy and golden brown. Serves 8.

ଔ

The name "jackass corn" is indicative of the fact that, like a jackass or a workhorse, this is hard, crispy, and sweet, but stubborn—a tough cookie to beat!

Macaroni and Cheese

1	tbsp. butter or oil		1	cup New York aged cheddar cheese, shredded
1	lb. elbow macaroni, cooked and drained		1	cup Monterey Jack cheese, shredded
1	stick butter		1	cup Velveeta cheese
4	tbsp. flour		2	eggs, beaten
2	cups half and half		2	tbsp. clarified butter
Salt and pepper, optional			4	tbsp. herb-flavored breadcrumbs
1	cup Muenster cheese, shredded		½	cup Parmesan cheese
1	cup sharp cheddar, shredded			

Preheat oven to 350° F. Grease casserole with 1 tablespoon of butter or oil. In a large sauté pan, add the butter and flour, stirring constantly to form a roux. Stir in the milk and slowly bring to boiling. Remove from heat. Add salt and pepper, if desired. Stir in the cheeses, macaroni, and slowly stir in the eggs. Transfer the mixture to the baking dish. Bake for 30 minutes. Top with a mixture of the clarified butter, bread crumbs, and Parmesan cheese. Bake for 10 minutes more. The crust should now be temptingly golden, but cool for 15 minutes before serving. Serves 8.

☙

Comfort … talk about comfort food! You will not be thinking of anything else at that moment; time stands still while you're eating this dish.

Roasting Breadfruit

Jamaica is blessed with the "yellow heart" breadfruit. It is the most sought-after starchy fruit, and is best served when roasted. Roasting may be done in a regular oven, on the burner of a gas stove, in a microwave oven, or on the grill or outdoor fire. It may also be boiled, eaten like a potato, or used in salads.

Here are a few roasting tips: Remove the stem. Use a sharp, pointed knife to pierce directly into the center; slash an X at the bottom to release some steam while baking. Bake in oven at 350° F for 30 to 45 minutes. When done, the skin is dark brown and soft to the touch. On a gas-stove burner, charcoal fire, or grill, rotate the fruit every 10 minutes, until the skin becomes dark or black all around. When done this way, some like to eat the skin, but first, scrape with a sharp knife to remove the black crust, leaving a smooth brown crust. Roasting may also be done in a microwave oven. Bake on high for 20-30 minutes, depending on size of the fruit. Peel and remove skin before serving. Slice and serve with butter or other accompaniments.

Scalloped Potatoes

6   medium potatoes, peeled and sliced

4   tbsp. butter

2   onions, peeled and sliced

4   tbsp. flour

1   tsp. seasoning salt

1   scotch bonnet pepper, minced (no seeds)

1   tsp. fresh thyme leaves

1   12-oz. can evaporated milk

1   cup water

½   cup grated cheese, bacon, or ham chunks

Garnish: blades of chives

Preheat oven to 350° F. Grease or spray a 12-inch by 9-inch casserole dish. In a large saucepan, add the potatoes, cover with water, bring to a boil, and cook for 3 minutes. Drain and set aside. Heat the butter in a saucepan; sauté the onions, stir in the flour, seasoning salt, pepper, and thyme. Slowly add the milk, stirring to form a roux. Remove from heat. Layer the potatoes in the baking dish and pour the roux over it. Sprinkle cheese or bacon or ham or all three ingredients. Bake for 25 minutes until potatoes are golden. Serves 8.

ଔ

With the addition of bacon or ham, this may well fit in as a one-pot meal. Decorate with chives and serve with grace.

Seasoned Rice

1   lb. codfish

4   cups water

1   17-oz. canned ackee, drained

1   cup pumpkin, diced

1   onion, minced

3   stalks escallion (green onion), chopped

3   sprigs thyme

3   cloves garlic, minced

2   cups coconut milk

1   scotch bonnet pepper, minced, seeds removed

1   plum tomato, diced

4   cups rice

1   cup cabbage, diced

Soak codfish overnight, drain, flake, and set aside. Bring 4 cups water to a boil. Add ackee, pumpkin, onion, escallion (green onion), thyme, and garlic and return to a boil. Add coconut milk, codfish, pepper, tomatoes, and rice. Bring to a boil. Add cabbage, cover and simmer on low heat for 20 minutes, until rice is steam-cooked. Test the rice grains for doneness, and add small amounts of water, if needed. Fluff rice. Serves 8.

ଓ

Experience this delightful one-pot meal, which may also be served as a side dish.

Stuffed Turkey Dressing

1   cup celery, chopped

1   onion, minced

½   cup butter

5   cups cornbread stuffing mix

2   cups Fuji apples, cored and cubed

1   cup tomatoes, chopped

2   cooked sausages, chopped

1   cup broth

1   orange, zest

½   cup orange juice

1   tsp. fresh thyme leaves

Seasoning salt to taste

1   scotch bonnet pepper

In a heatproof casserole over low heat, melt the butter, celery, and onion. Stir while adding the cornbread stuffing, apples, tomatoes, sausages, broth, zest, juice, thyme leaves, salt, and pepper. If mixture gets too dry, add more broth. Fluff with a fork to keep from clumping. Stuff the turkey just before roasting.

℘

Some prefer not to stuff their turkey. If desired, this dressing may be baked in a 350° F oven for about 45 minutes.

Spicy Pocket Dictionary

with briefs-tales-tips

As a curious child, I overheard and stored in memory gobs of awesome tales, secretive and risqué conversations held by my elderly relatives. Had I been caught eavesdropping, I would not ably tell any tales now. Little did I know that remarks like, "dis will put it back," or "dis will put vim in ya voom," meant that certain foods have aphrodisiac properties and health benefits. Somehow the risqué connotations added the extra flair and alerted my senses.

Designed especially for your reading pleasure is my compilation of foods used or mentioned in this book with related briefs—tales—tips and some hidden quips. Now that I have your interest piqued—let go of any inhibitions—assess and judge for yourself.

Aphrodisiacs
Other Food and Spices
Come to Terms
Help Is On The Way
Abbreviations
Bar Measures
"Guesstimated" Food Measures
Substitutions
Weights and Measures

Aphrodisiacs

Apples: The fruits of the tree of good and evil—Eve ripped them off, tempted Adam—he ate the whole thing.

Bananas: Name it—they contain healthy fiber, vitamins, potassium, and is rumored to stave off impotence … a sexy fruit to befriend.

Beans: Behind Every Ass Nuff Sounds—who cares, when beans are high in protein, and proteins are libido enhancers.

Callaloo: Loaded with iron for stamina.

Carrots: Contain carotene or vitamin A for good eyesight, among other sights.

Cayenne: Helps heal ulcers of the stomach and colon, and stimulates a heart to love.

Cheeses: Think "libido" and cheese is a turn-on; think "sex" and again cheese to the rescue. Think comfort as in the soft taste of Camembert cheese, or try any cheese that you fancy, any place, anytime, for all occasions, just say "cheese" and snap away.

Chocolate: The food of love with its afterglow effects; be it all in the brain. Endorphins in the brain erupt, making you mindful of some good feelings of being in love, taking you beyond to the loving after the loving.

Coffee: Such an aphrodisiac that boosts libido, stamina, and desire—keeps you awake, alive and kicking for more.

Garlic: Works like an antibiotic to promote health, strength, stamina, and virility.

Ginger: Absorbs toxins, assists digestion, relieves nausea, and stimulates libido.

Ginseng: The tea made from this root promotes endurance and puts "vim in your voom."

Grapes: Wild or otherwise, they do not have to turn into wine to do the trick.

Honey: Loosen up with a tongue-full of this aphrodisiac between you and your honey.

Kumquats: Stimulates and spikes the taste buds, even the lips are a kissable territory.

Mangoes: How it is eaten does not alter its potential. Dice it, slice it, lick it, suck it, serve it to your mate; from your lips to his, the rewards are immense pleasure while it keeps the juices flowing.

Meats: Heighten the human animal instincts.

Mint: Peppermint, spearmint, or catmint; variety is the spice of life; a potential aphrodisiac used in teas or salads, and leaves your breath tasting good.

Nutmeg: Keep one in the pocket to disperse a curse. Suck on a piece of nutmeg to prevent nausea. Wards off impotence. Used in drinks, it is believed to prevent premature ejaculation, but could become addictive.

Parsley: Keeps bad breath away. Encourages kissing.

Peanuts: Heighten sexuality—nuts do that.

Pumpkin seeds: They do something for the libido.

Saffron: Keeps the joints in good condition, eases bone ache.

Seafood: Oysters—aphrodisiac extraordinaire! Don't ignore the potency in conch, scallops, shrimps, and fish, which stimulate the brain. Remember that lovemaking requires brainwork.

Soursop: Feeling nervous? The nectar from this fruit will put your "deck of cards" in a "straight flush." Get the picture?

Spinach: Perks up the eyesight for anyone peeking through holes—keyholes, that is. Has a high iron content, which fosters stamina and longevity.

Strawberries: Be a tease; feed your mate strawberries dipped in melted chocolate; candidly speaking, allow the chocolate to ooze all over his lips and yours.

Turmeric: Pain reliever—libido lifter.

Vanilla beans: Used in scented bath preparations and love potions for enticing the opposite sex. The beans give an extra kick to ice cream, among other things.

Whipping cream: Soak in a heavenly milk bath after a workout or a marathon—angelic beings will be there to soothe and calm those tired, aching bodies. You'll be floating on cloud 9.

Wines and spirits: To toast all fears away—out of the issues of the spirit the mouth speaks.

Other Foods and Spices

Ackee: The ackee tree was brought to Jamaica from West Africa in the 1700's. However, because of its classification as a poisonous fruit, the fist-sized, coral-red pods must be allowed to ripen and burst open on the tree to release the harmful gases. The pod opens into three segments, revealing three pieces of yellow fruit, each having a red membrane in the center and a shiny black seed, which must be removed and discarded. Wash and cook the fruit until tender; drain and discard the water, then prepare as suggested by the recipe of choice. The fruit, when prepared as ackee and saltfish, has the appearance of scrambled eggs; makes an exquisite pair, when teamed up with the famous roasted breadfruit, and enjoyed by foreigners and locals. It is renowned as Jamaica's national dish.

Allspice—pimento: The grains or berries are picked green, dried, and used whole or ground as a spice for jerking meats and fish, in curries, soups, stews, pickles, and the ripe berries used to manufacture pimento liqueur. Pimento leaf oil is extracted from the leaves for export and used in restaurants. The wood gives a unique smoke flavor to meats cooked on outdoor grills. The plant is related to cloves and the bay leaf tree.

Anise: This is of the parsley family, with a yellowish-white flower, yielding an aromatic aniseed. Dried star anise offers a spicy, licorice-like flavor—one of the ingredients in Chinese five-spice powder used in stews.

Annatto: Annatto grows in the West Indies and may be found in most tropical countries. The plant yields bunches of hairy, rusty-red seedpods. When dried, the seeds are a deep orange-rust-red color, often stored in oil, used as food coloring for sauces, gravies, soups, or ground and used as a spice like saffron or turmeric in curries and baking.

Avocado: In Jamaica, "pear" is the common name for an avocado. Also known as "poor man's butter," this bland-tasting fruit has many essential vitamins and is very low in saturated fat. Two very popular varieties are the green-skin, thick-fruity "Simmons," and the purple-skin, long-necked "alligator" pear. Whether sliced, diced, added to salads, or blended with onion, escallion (green onion), pepper, lemon juice, and salt to make a guacamole dip, avocado pear is an excellent sandwich spread on bulla or bread. In Jamaica, at functions or family gatherings, one might hear this comical cheering expression, in agreement to what is said, "Hear! Hear! Bread and pear!"

Banana: Jamaica has a wide variety of bananas. The most popular are the Gros Michel or Lacatan. Green bananas may be boiled and eaten as a carbohydrate, fried or baked as chips, ripened for fruit, or baked as a dessert, and when preserved in a dehydrator, it is referred to as a banana fig. Bananas are loaded with dietary fiber, vitamin B, and very rich in potassium. It is known to help calm emotions, moodiness, and nervousness; to neutralize over-acidity in the stomach; to regulate blood glucose level; as a cooling agent in the body; and especially to stave off impotence. Yes! Look at those raised eyebrows!

Bay leaves: Taken from the bay tree and used in soups, stews, fish, and for medicinal purposes.

Birds: Baldpate or doves are smaller birds than the quail or Cornish hen. Birds are a delicacy. They are usually cleaned, seasoned whole, and tenderized by soaking in milk or precooking for 15 minutes prior to frying, baking, or roasting.

Breadfruit: Captain Bligh introduced the breadfruit tree to Jamaica in the 1700's. It is quite a beautiful tree, with large green, glossy, finger-like leaves. As kids, we tied the yellow ripe leaves to our feet as make-believe slippers; we punctured the bark of the tree to extract the sap, which, when coagulated, was our chewing gum. The sword-like blossoms may be preserved. One variety, the "yellow heart," is especially sumptuous when allowed to almost ripen, roasted, baked or fried and served with ackee and saltfish. The young fruit is cooked and eaten like potatoes, or used in salads.

Callaloo: A substitute for spinach, nicknamed "greens" and used in pepper pot soup. Makes a very soulful combination with onions, tomatoes, and coconut milk. Referred to as "ital" in the Rastafarian circle. Serve steamed or stir-fried with saltfish or mackerel rundown.

Cardamom: An Asian spice used as a sweet flavouring for pastries.

Cashew: A tropical fruit with a nut-seed at the opposite end of the stem. The fruit has a tangy taste, rich in iron, and makes an excellent preserve, wine, or juice. The seed is roasted to remove the nut from a thick, oil-based shell, which exudes a toxic substance, harmful and blinding to farm-raised chickens. I recall the strict measures taken by my grandparents to protect their chickens each cashew-roasting season.

Cassava or Bammy: This tuber comes in two varieties, the sweet and the bitter cassava. The bitter cassava is used for the production of starch. The sweet variety is used mainly for food, from which Bammy is made.

Cayenne: Tiny, red, hot, chili peppers. I know them as bird peppers, and as the name implies, birds love them. Use them whole, or dried and ground, for spicing salads, soups, meats, or seafood.

Chinese Bean Paste: Black soybean paste, or red bean curd can be found in Chinese specialty stores or regular supermarkets.

Chinese five-spice powder (Ng Heung Fun): A blend of five or more spices, including cinnamon, pepper, ginger, cloves, fennel, star anise, and dried tangerine peel.

Chinese Mushrooms (Dtung Goo): These are dried, and therefore need to be soaked in water to soften, before cooking with meat or vegetable dishes.

Chinese Oyster Sauce (Hoi Yu): Adds flavour to meats, vegetables, and fried rice.

Chinese Sausage (Fah Chung): Needs to be steamed, sliced diagonally, and served as a side dish with baby sweet onions or diced and added to fried rice.

Chives: A small version of escallion (green onion) with a tubular leaf and the taste of onions or garlic. Use the leaves as an herb when preparing soups, salads, sauces, or dips, and as a garnish.

Cho-cho or chayote: A member of the gourd family, this green or white prickly, furrowed, pear-shaped squash grows on a strong vine; a bland-tasting vegetable used in soups, stews, pickles, and as an accompaniment with fish and meats.

Cilantro: Otherwise known as Chinese parsley or coriander. The leaves have a strong taste and smell, and rumor has it that it was named after the bedbug. But, the good qualities far outweigh the bad. Use the seeds in potpourri, and enjoy the leaves on salads or soups or as a garnish for sauces. It also reduces bad breath.

Cinnamon: A sweet-tasting, fragrant bark of the cinnamon tree, which may be bought as stick or powdered cinnamon to be used when baking pastries or cakes. The leaves are also full of flavor and may be used to add zest to cereals, chocolate drinks, and teas.

Citrus: Consist of citron, grapefruits, lemons, limes, sweet limes, sweet oranges, Seville or sour oranges, ortaniques (which is a cross between a tangerine and an orange), pommelo or shaddock, tangerines and kumquats or cumquats. In Jamaica, most of these are popularly grown and used in preserves; some are scant.

Cloves: Dried flower buds from a tropical tree, used as a spice when baking ham, in soups, stews, and desserts.

Coco: A starchy tuber, like dasheen, serves well in soups. It's easily digestible, soft enough to mash like potatoes, and fed to babies.

Cocoa: Produced from the cocoa bean to make chocolate, cocoa powder, or rolled into balls to make chocolate tea or drink.

Coconuts: The green coconut water is a popular drink or chaser for strong drinks, usually referred to as rum and coconut water. But never confuse coconut water with coconut milk. The milk is extracted from the flesh of the dry coconut and used in sauces, stews, curried dishes, rice and peas, ice cream, or piña colada. The flesh is grated or shredded and used in salads, cakes, toppings, and candies.

Curry powder: Blended pungent spices, consisting of turmeric, cayenne pepper, black pepper, ginger, saffron, allspice, annatto, coriander seeds, fenugreek seeds, cumin, mustard, nutmeg, cinnamon, and star anise, create a variety of flavours and colours of golden yellow to orange-yellow curry powder for use in stews, gravies, sauces, and the much-loved Jamaican curried goat.

Garlic: Pungent bulb having several cloves. Used as a seasoning for meats, soups, sauces, gravies, and has healing antibiotic properties.

Ginger: Grown in Jamaica and used as a spice in cakes, sweets, drinks, preserves, and as a tea. Jamaica produces the best-tasting ginger beer. Ginger relieves indigestion and travel sickness; some believe it wards off impotence.

Guava: When ripe, this round or pear-shaped, greenish-yellow, thin-skinned fruit, has a yellow or pink flesh with seeds condensed in the center. The fruit has its own pectin, a necessary jellying agent used in preserves, jams, or jellies. Preserved guava shells, guava cheese, guava jelly, guava wine, or drink are some favorites.

Indian kale: Belongs to the dasheen or coco family. The leaves are mixed with callaloo or spinach and added to pepperpot soup, or served like any other green leafy vegetable.

June plum: The ripe fruits are 2 to 3 inches long, greenish-yellow in color, sweet but sour enough to induce a mouth-watering effect on the taste buds. Peel away the skin—exposing a firm, juicy flesh covering a fibrous, spiny seed. The fruit may be used in salads, chutneys, jams, preserves, juices, and wines.

Kumquats: Little plum-sized orange-like citrus fruits. Taste delightful in preserves, marmalades, and drinks.

Lemongrass: This is called fever grass in Jamaica. It is used to make a tea, and is known for its herbal benefits. In some Asian cuisine, it is used to enhance the flavor of soups and stews.

Mango: This fruit is one of the most loved, most exquisite and exotic desserts served in Jamaica, and talk about variety; there are myriads of names, colors, textures, sweetness, and even the hairiness is a turn-on. Mangoes are passionately loaded fruits—served alone or with a scoop of ice cream—you will be asking what's the scoop!

Naseberry: Also called the sapodilla. The fruit is brown-colored with a sandy feel to the skin. The flesh is pinkish-brown and succulently sweet. Eat only when ripe. It makes a delicious addition to salads. The trees also produce a gum used to make chewing gum.

Okra: The plant is a member of the hibiscus family, grows to a height of two to four feet, and bears a horny finger-like vegetable, used in pepperpot gumbo, stews, or served as a side dish with fish.

Otaheite apples: These pear-shaped, cerise to ruby- or wine-red apples have one large stone or seed with a mildly scented, pure white, juicy, edible fruit. May also be stewed, preserved, or juiced.

Paprika: Sweet red pepper powder used in meat dishes, vegetables, and soups, or as a decorative garnish on deviled eggs, potato or macaroni salads.

Passion fruit: Grows on a vine that sends out purple blooms and matures into a fruit with a hard shell. When cut open, there are many black seeds with a pulpy covering. This is sometimes sour to taste, but to counteract that, the seeds are mixed with water, passed through a sieve, and sweetened with condensed milk or sugar to make a delightful drink. Other related fruits are the "sweet cup" and the "grand Della."

Peas, beans: There are a few varieties, each having its own character, protein content, and usefulness. The red kidney beans, the black eyed peas, or the gungo peas may be used green or dried, to make stews, soups, or rice and peas. Lima or broad beans are used mainly in stews. String beans, long beans, or snow peas are steamed, stir-fried with any meat, used in casseroles, or served as a vegetable. Mung beans make excellent bean sprouts. Soybeans are high in protein and may be cooked and eaten green or used to make a bean curd, bean paste, or tofu. The list is endless, a loaded food group.

Peppercorn: True peppercorn is harvested from a climbing vine grown in the jungles of southern India. Peppercorns were very expensive in the middle ages and were often used as money for dowries or to pay taxes and rent. The demand for spices—black pepper being one of the most highly used spices, led to a multitude of voyages, the discovery and competitiveness between the European states. Now peppercorns of various colors are found in gourmet markets around the world.

Plantains: Related to the banana, but a larger variety. Green plantains may be used to make chips, baked, boiled, roasted, or grated to make porridge. When partially ripened, it may be steam-baked in the microwave oven, and the fully ripened fruit may be baked, fried, or used to make plantain tarts.

Scotch bonnet pepper: Has a rich golden yellow or green color—shaped like a bonnet—hot as hell— no one need go there. Remove and toss the seeds and veins—the outer skin is hot enough. Should you choose to devour the seeds—they could hurt you twice! You were forewarned—wash your hands thoroughly or wear protective gloves.

Sea grapes: These trees grow wild, mainly found along the sea or coastal areas. The grapes are sweetish-salty-tangy and are used in jams and jellies.

Sorrel: The plant belongs to the hibiscus family and bears seed-buds with bright red sepals, which mature at Christmastime. The sepals are used to make a drink, usually served at every Christmas table.

Soursop: This fruit is heart shaped with spiky, green skin. The soft, pulpy flesh is pure white with black seeds, which must be removed when extracting the nectar. Other related fruits are the sweetsop and custard apple.

Star apple: As the name suggests, this fruit looks like a star when cut on the cross section. It grows in two varieties, one is green and the other is purple-colored. When ripe, the fruit is soft to the touch. The large black seeds are removed and the jelly-like pulp is eaten alone or combined with orange or grapefruit segments and condensed milk to create a dessert called "matrimony."

Sugarcane: Sugar plantations and sugar factories were once an economic boost for Jamaica. Sugar, molasses, and rum are still produced here, but in smaller quantities.

Susumber: Known as gully bean in Jamaica, and related to the garden eggplant or aubergine. The plant produces bunches of seeds, very much like green peas in shape and color, but slightly bitter-tasting when cooked. They are most palatable if picked before maturity and prepared with salted codfish.

Tamarind: This legume or beanlike fruit is encased in a brown seedpod or shell. When ripe, the shell is easily removed, revealing a brown, clammy, pulpy, sticky, mouth-watering, sweet-and-sour fruit, used to make preserves, chutneys, drinks, or rolled in sugar to form tamarind balls.

Pumpkin: The most sought-after variety in Jamaica is the curry pumpkin, so named because of the golden, orange-yellow color it gives to soups, polenta, rice dishes, and more. It is best if mature, dry, and firm in texture.

Thyme: A pungent spice or herb used to enhance flavors in cooking soups, meats, fish, and known to help relieve a cough or cold.

Turmeric: A rhizome, like ginger—used for its color and flavor—one of the ingredients in curry powder—used in place of saffron. It is believed to have anti-inflammatory effect in relieving arthritic pain.

Vanilla: The climbing vine produces vanilla beans, and from the beans a vanilla extract is made. Vanilla is used in cakes, pies, puddings, ice cream, sweets, and drinks.

Yam: A starchy root with varied color, taste, and texture. When cooked, some yams are soft, firm, or waxy, and may be served with meats, added to soups, or used like a potato in salads.

Come to Terms

Appeteasers: Appetizers

Bake: Cooking with dry heat in an oven, on heated metal, bricks, or stones.

Barbecue: Broiling, grilling, or roasting over hot charcoal.

Baste: To moisten meat or food during cooking with pan drippings, butter, juices, sauces, or oils to enhance flavor and retain juiciness.

Batter: A mixture of flour, eggs, milk, and water, beaten together to make pancakes or used to coat foods before frying.

Beat: Whisking or stirring briskly and vigorously with a fork or in a blender to make a mixture light, airy, and smooth.

Blanch: To immerse food in boiling water for a short time, then suddenly dunk it into ice-cold water to halt the cooking process. Prepare for freezing.

Blend: Mix of ingredients to form an inseparable and smooth combination.

Braise: Cooking meats, fish, or vegetables by sautéing in fat then simmering in a small amount of liquid.

Brawta: Bartering for more at the end of a deal; asking for extras, bonus, or tip.

Brew: To make beer, coffee, or tea.

Brisket: Meat from the breast portion of the cow, with cartilage, or gristle, and used in stew.

Broil: Grilling or cooking by direct heat under a broiler or on a gridiron.

Brown: To cook, roast, fry, or sauté to a brown color.

Browning: Used in one of my recipes as a play on words to describe a brownie. Browning is a dark form of molasses or burnt sugar, used in plum puddings or dark cakes.

Caramelize: Convert by melting sugar to form a sauce, glaze, or syrup.

Casserole: Covered pottery or dish used for baking a mixture of food.

Chill: Refrigerate to make cool.

Chop: To mince or cut in pieces with a knife, scissors, or chopper.

Clarify: To skim or remove fat from soup stock, broth, or butter, leaving a clear liquid.

Coat: To dip food in batter, egg, bread crumbs, or nuts, to form a cover or coating.

Coffee-fy: To gratify one's love for coffee.

Coffee cubes: Frozen leftover coffee.

Compote: Fruit cooked or stewed in syrup. Dessert served in stemmed glass compote.

Condiment: Food flavoring like ketchup, mustard, and spices.

Cream: Butter and sugar, creamed together to form a smooth paste.

Crisp or Crispy: To cook, toast, or bake food until a firm crust is formed, or to immerse vegetables in ice water, until crunchy.

Crystallize: Coating and preserving fruit in sugar.

Cube: To cut food into approximately half-inch squares.

Crimp: Pinching the edges of a pastry crust or pressing with the tines of a fork to create a seal or a design.

Curing: Preserving meats or fish by smoking, drying, or salting in brine made with spices and saltpeter.

Cut in: Using a pastry cutter or two knives to chop or mix solid butter and flour to make a crust.

Dash: Approximately one-eighth of a teaspoonful or a pinch of a substance such as salt.

Degrease: The removal of fat from the top of soups, stock, stews, or gravies.

Dice: To cut into small squares or fine bits.

Dredge: Lightly coating food with flour or cornmeal.

Entree: The main course.

Fold: Mixing ingredients in a bowl using a spoon, spatula, or scraper with a lift upward, over, and under action.

Foreplay: My foreword is referred to as foreplay, indicative that I enjoy playing with words, not meaning to be disrespectful to the English language.

Garnish: Decorating main dishes with sprigs of thyme, rosemary, parsley, escallion (green onion), lemon slices, mint leaves; adding beauty and a finishing touch.

Grate: To reduce food to small particles by rubbing against a sharp pointed surface, as in grating a carrot or nutmeg.

Grease: To coat griddle irons, baking pans, casserole dishes, and skillets with oil or butter to prevent foods from sticking.

Grind: Using a grinder or a mill to reduce to fine particles, as in coffee—similar to grating.

Intercourse: Another one of my play on words, as in my main course or entree.

Jigger: A measure of spirits or wine, equal to three tablespoons.

Julienne: To cut vegetables, fruit and cheese into thin strips or matchstick-shaped slivers.

Knead: Working dough using the heel of the hands, with a folding, pushing, pressing, and punching-down pressure.

Marinate: Allowing food to stand in a marinade, sauce, or liquid spices, to soak up the seasonings or become tenderized.

Mince: To chop finely, smaller than dicing.

Nuff-nuff: Plenty, in abundance.

Panther: A brand name, "wear your panther," for safe sex.

Parch: Cooking without water to a dry state, without burning.

Peel: To remove the skin or outer covering of fruits, food, and vegetables.

Pot-roast: Cooking meat in a covered Dutch pot.

Preserve: Boiling fruit with sugar to make jams.

Punch down: Hand a fist to raised bread dough.

Puree: Food blended into a smooth paste.

Reduce: To cook or boil liquid until concentrated or thickened.

Roast: To cook meat in an oven with dry heat.

Roll: Referred to as "rolling out the dough," using a rolling pin to flatten out a biscuit or pastry crust.

Sauté: Pan-frying meat or vegetables in butter or oil, until browned and cooked.

Scald: Heating milk to boiling point.

Score: Shallow slits, openings or designs made with a sharp knife on ham, fish, meat, or other foods.

Sear: Browning meats with intense heat to seal in flavors and juices.

Shred: Food cut or torn in slivers or thin slices using a knife or a shredder.

Sliver: A small, narrow, sharp piece of food, split or cut off a larger piece (a sliver of cheese).

Simmer: Cooking in liquid, low heat, bringing it to a slow, rippling boil.

Steep: Tea or fruit drinks made with boiled water, covered and left to stand for a few minutes.

Stew: To cook, simmer, or boil on slow heat.

Stir: To mix with a circular motion while blending liquids or soft substances.

Stir-fry: A method of cooking and stirring food with oil in a wok, frying pan, or skillet.

Supreme: The term "supreme" as in "supreme an orange," applies to cutting away the rind, membranes, and seeds of any citrus fruit, extracting perfectly supreme segments, perfect for any dessert compote, fruit salads, marmalades, or preserves.

Toast: Brown or make crisp in a toaster oven.

Whip or whisk: To beat rapidly with a beater or a whisk, incorporating air to fluff and make egg whites form peaks.

Zest: The outer layer of an orange or citrus in general, often removed with a peeler or a grater.

Help Is on the Way

Anytime, anywhere, always have baking soda on hand—it's like having a pharmacy in a box. It is great for relieving stomach upset, heartburn, and indigestion, soothing for burns, insect bites, and itching skin.

Baking soda works efficiently as a household deodorizer that absorbs odors throughout the home. It's a safe cleaner without harsh abrasives or toxic chemicals, for washing fruits, scouring the kitchen sink, countertop, stovetop, oven, dishwasher, pots, pans, glassware, silverware, jewelry, bathrooms, and innumerable first aid uses.

Beans are known to help keep the arteries unclogged—eat them regularly—excellent source of protein.

Beans may be cooked and frozen twenty-four hours before use, to reduce the gas content.

Before grilling meats, cut several slits along the fat edge to prevent meat from curling.

Blister is gone—within the first few hours after getting a mild burn, soak the area in very cold milk to avoid a blister.

Brush some oil on meat after seasonings are added, to hold in the flavors and prevent it from sticking to the grill or pan.

Charcoal or chalk help keep rust out of your toolbox.

Charcoal, finely ground, may be used for cleaning teeth.

Charcoal capsules may be bought at the pharmacy and taken for cleansing the stomach.

Chopped escallion (green onion), stored in the freezer, reduces spoilage and comes in handy on a "rainy day."

Cornmeal may be used to scrub away blemishes on the skin.

Dumplings and spinners may be shaped or rolled while holding the hands over the pot of soup or stew—the steam generated from the pot keeps the dough smooth and less crumbly.

Eating egg yolks is known to preserve vision.

Eating spinach works wonders for the eyesight.

Eggs placed in cold water, then brought to boiling, are less likely to crack.

Eggs placed in very cold water immediately after boiling will peel smoothly—smash the shell all around and remove under cold running water.

For plump raisins in cakes, soak them in warm water before adding to mixture.

Fruit-flavored woodchips, spices, and herbs may be added to charcoal to give meats a special smoke flavor. Some examples are: allspice (pimento), cinnamon, citrus, cloves, cumin, dill, nutmeg, oregano, thyme, and tealeaves.

Garlic or onions smell on your hands, even after washing with lemon juice—try rubbing your hands over aluminum foil or your metal kitchen sink—the smell is "a goner!"

Green onion flowers: cut green onion stalks into two-inch pieces. Cut almost halfway down each stalk, and set in ice-cold water until the ends curl beautifully. Vary your design by cutting one-third down both ends of the stalks and have both ends curling.

Honey is useful as a facial mask—add to that some lemon juice and allow the astringent to work wonders tightening the skin—feels as smooth as a baby's bottom!

If diced onions are unpleasant to taste in salads, try using the whole onion or cut it in halves or quarters. Mix in with the salad to retain the flavor, but be sure to remove before serving.

If soups, stews, or sauces are burned during cooking, quickly remove from heat and pour into a clean cookware without stirring. Chutneys and flavorings may be added to mask the burnt taste, if any.

Keep weevils out of flour, beans, grains, etc., by storing them in the refrigerator or in glass jars.

Lemon juice repels ants, leaving a sour taste in their mouths.

Lime or lemon juice, squeezed over fruits or food, will prevent discoloration.

Make the odious task of scaling fish easier by soaking them in salty water for a few minutes. The scales curl away making clean up a cinch.

Pistachio nuts are sometimes difficult to crack open—no need to throw them out—pry with half of a husk placed between the crack of the whole nut—works like a snap.

Raw salads eaten before the main meal help digestion of protein and other foods, and lessen the chances of overeating.

Repel ants in the kitchen with a mixture of flour, cinnamon, and vinegar.

Ripe banana peel helps relieve itching caused by insect bites or poison ivy.

Rub cooking oil on your barbecue grill rack to prevent foods from sticking to it.

Rub parsley on mosquito bites to relieve the itching.

Rub soap on the outside of your pots and pans before cooking on an outdoor wood or charcoal fire, and smoke stains will wash off easily.

Rust stains on your kitchen towels may be removed by soaking and rubbing with a solution of lime juice, salt, and baking soda.

Salt removes wine stains from a white tablecloth.

Stash a box of baking soda in your freezer, refrigerator, or kitchen cupboards to help absorb food odors. Do not use the same box for cooking. Change every month or two.

Stains on fine china may be removed with a soft cloth, ice-cold water, lime juice, and salt.

Store leftover foods in glass containers in the refrigerator to restrain odors.

Toss those used tea bags into your rose garden for healthier and more beautiful blooms.

215

Toss used coffee grinds into the garden—it repels pests and pets, while acting as a fertilizer to the plants.

Try a cool tea bag to soothe tired, puffy eyes.

Try ginger tea to soothe a sore throat; it does great for indigestion too.

Use frozen coffee cubes to chill and enhance your iced cappuccino or other iced coffee drinks, instead of ice, which dilutes the coffee.

Vinegar, diluted with water, is a wonder cleaner for tile floors. Leaves them glowing and glossy.

Vinegar is an effective deodorizer for pots and pans. A few drops in boiling water will remove fishy odors from cookware.

Vinegar mixed with equal parts of dishwashing liquid and water help remove stains from fabric.

Vinegar is excellent for removing calcium build-up in the coffeepot or teakettle. Allow the vinegar to boil in the relevant container for a few minutes, and watch as the calcium magically disappears.

When baking, mix fruits and nuts with dry ingredients, to prevent them from falling to the bottom of the pan.

When buying grapefruits and oranges, feel for the heavier ones; they are usually juicier.

When grilling steaks, timing is important. For juicy steaks, turn only once, allowing 3 to 5 minutes on the first side, then 8 minutes for rare and 10 minutes for medium on the other side. The thickness of the steak determines the cooking time, for example, a tenderloin ¾ inch thick would take 7 to 9 minutes, or 1 inch thick would take 10 to 12 and up to 14 minutes.

Nothing like a good rump! Rump roast, of course! Suggestion for roasting meats to perfection, every time, is the use of a meat thermometer. Basically, allow approximately 30 minutes' cooking time per pound of meat. Test meat for doneness—internal temperatures indicate rare at 140° F, medium at 160° F and well done at 170° F.

Wit or wisdom—but me no buts! Here are some excellent tips on selecting lean cuts of beef, which contain the least amounts of fat and cholesterol. In the rear end—eye of round, top round (London broil), tip roast or tip steaks. In the loin area, there's the top sirloin, tenderloin (filet mignon), T-bone, and porterhouse steaks. Do not be afraid to use the loin chops or the rib roast, grilled or roasted; be sure to allow the fat to melt then drain off. Now as we move forward into the chuck area—there we have the seven-bone roast, the shoulder blade roast or steaks.

Whatever your meat selection, I encourage safe cooking and handling techniques; using antibacterial cleansers for the hands and for keeping the kitchen spotlessly clean—the key to a healthy lifestyle as you "Do It In The Kitchen."

Abbreviations

lb. = pound

ml = milliliter

oz. = ounce

pkg. = package

qt. = quart

tsp. = teaspoon

tbsp. = tablespoon

Bar Measures

dash = 1/32 oz.

1/8 oz. = 1 tsp.

3/8 oz. = 1 tbsp.

1 oz. = 1 pony

1½ oz. = 1 jigger

4 oz. = 1 wine glass

6 oz. = 1 split

8 oz. = 1 cup

"Guesstimated" Food Measures

1 stick butter = ½ cup butter

1 cup shredded cheese = 4 oz. grated cheese

1 cup cream cheese = 8 oz. pkg. cream cheese

1 cup blue cheese = 4 oz. crumbled blue cheese

1 cup heavy cream = 2 cups whipped cream

1 lemon = ¼ cup or 3 tbsp. lemon juice

1 lemon = 1 tbsp. zest

1 lime = 1-2 tbsp. lime juice

1 lime = 1 tsp. zest

1 tsp. dried herb = 1 tbsp. fresh herb

1 stalk escallion (green onion) = 1 tbsp. escallion, chopped

1 stalk celery = 1/3 cup celery, chopped

1 sweet bell pepper = 1 cup pepper, diced

1 medium onion = ½ cup onion, minced

1 cup bread cubes = 2 slices toast

1 cup soft bread crumbs = 2 slices bread

1 cup dry bread crumbs = 4 slices toast

4 cups dry bread crumbs = 1 lb.

4 cups flour = 1 lb.

3 cups cornmeal = 1 lb.

2¼ cups brown sugar = 1 lb.

2 cups granulated sugar = 1 lb.

4 cups icing sugar = 1 lb.

2 cups rice = 14 oz.

Substitutions

4 cloves garlic = 1 tsp. garlic powder

1 cup sour cream = 3 tbsp. buttermilk and yogurt to fill a cup

1 cup whole milk = ½ cup evaporated milk and ½ cup water

1 cup buttermilk = 1 cup yogurt

1 cup yogurt = 1 cup warm milk and 1 tbsp. vinegar

1 oz. chocolate = 3 tbsp. cocoa powder and 2 tbsp. butter

1 cup self-rising flour = 1 cup flour, 2 tsp. baking powder + ½ tsp. salt

1 tbsp. cornstarch = 2 tbsp. flour

1 cup brown sugar = 1 cup granulated sugar

1 cup granulated sugar = 1 cup honey

1 cup corn syrup = ½ cup sugar

1 cup molasses = ¾ cup sugar

1 tbsp. lemon juice = 1 tbsp. white vinegar

2 egg yolks = 1 whole egg

1 cup tomato juice = ½ cup tomato sauce and ½ cup water

Weights and Measures

Dash = 1/8 tsp. liquid

Pinch = 1/8 tsp. salt

1½ tsp. = ¼ oz. = 7 ml

3 tsp. = ½ oz. = 1 tbsp.

2 tbsp. = 1 oz. = 30 ml

3 tbsp. = 1½ oz. = 1 jigger

4 tbsp. = ¼ cup = 2 oz.

5 tbsp. + 1 tsp. = 1/3 cup

8 tbsp. = ½ cup = 4 oz. = 125 ml

8 oz. = 1 cup = ½ pint = 250 ml

16 oz. (liquid) = 2 cups = 1 pint = 500 ml

3 cups = 750 ml = a fifth

4 cups = 32 oz. = 2 pints

2 pints   = 1 qt. = 1 liter

4 qt. (liquid) = 1 gallon

Picture, No Picture, Yes Picture!

223

229

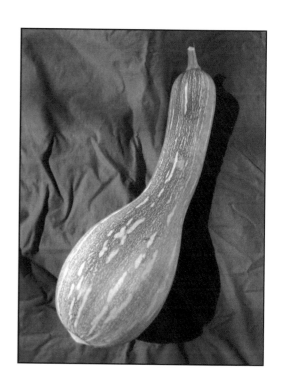

Index of Recipes

Who Is the Author?

There is a small farm located on the back roads of an obscure country village at Sign, Orange District, Saint James, Jamaica, where I spent my first sixteen years. Sign, as I recall, is a mere five-mile walk or ride from the city of Montego Bay, and until a highway runs through to replace or alter the route, I'm able to close my eyes and trace every curb, nook and cranny.

This cherry-red-cheek, half-Chinese damsel was known as the only "China gal" in the community, with innumerable farm duties to perform daily, before running two and a half miles to school. Yet, always chirpy like the birds, it reflected in my skipping, hopping, whistling, and laughing-all-the-time attitude.

As a farmer's granddaughter, I learned to improvise; turn my hands, so to speak, making small amounts of anything into plenty, without modern-day luxuries. As the old saying goes, "every mickle makes a muckle," and with many lessons in cooking on our brick fireside and baking in our brick oven, using wood to make fire coals; put to the test, I could still fit right in, cooking or baking the old-fashioned way. I could milk those cows and churn the butter manually, as if it were yesteryear. I'm extremely proud to have such strengths and resourcefulness to my credit. They are cherished assets that add affluence to my life.

Neither a frown nor scorn do I recall exhibiting, from having a heavier workload than my friends. During the summer vacation months, my cousins and friends would visit and spend weeks with me. This allowed me the freedom to share and convert my work into play; the joy of climbing and picking of the fruit trees; reaching for those luscious naseberries, guavas, guineps, June plums, or Otaheite apples more than compensated for the chores; my duties seemed lighter than a feather. Every waking moment was highly cherished, and when visitation time ended, I missed my visitors, but reverted to being my own company.

Like Tarzan and Jane in the jungle, I felt a oneness with nature, stomping around with the animal kingdom; penning the calves on time so their mothers gave us milk next morning; ensuring that the chickens were safely nestled in their roost, and collecting eggs for breakfast; bringing in the goats at dusk to sleep near the cellar, close to the kitchen corner, where they would be protected from thieves at night; hunting birds with a catapult or setting a cage (called a collar band) to catch them alive. Bird hunting was my father's summer ritual, and I inherited that trait. As an avid bird hunter today, I make no apologies for my make-up.

My grandparents taught me to develop a sound backbone with a positive approach to life; never be threatened by hard work; live with adversity and burst forth smelling like a rose; even Jesus came from obscurity to being God of the Universe. Some kids gossiped that I lived the "life of Riley" in a great house; some called me a "cocky" teenager. Undeniably, I have always been as sprightly spirited as the rooster or a "cock" as we say in Jamaican lingo. As it were, by the Chinese zodiac, being born the year of the cock, and being part Chinese, I embrace the fact that I am a cock by nature, but absolutely deny being cocky. My humble roots do render me proud.

One of my peers in the workplace conferred on me a nickname, Desiderata, insisting that she saw in me a quiet awareness, working under pressure without disheveling or ruffling feathers. She set out to imitate my style. Nicknames were unacceptable for me, but this was one exception. Desiderata signify peace and humility and encourage my choice for obscurity. So much so that I admonish everyone to seek and find your measure of peace in humility. My life is joyfully obscure, that of a self-propelled chef with no accolades, and a humble artist with no intention to bloviate.

My grandparents as chums, not prudes, made risqué remarks, always with good taste, not meant to offend, but lighten the air, placing smiles on everyone's face! They imparted their best to me, saying: "Only the best is good enough." Now here's to you, some of my best—Nuff Respect!

Printed in the United States
96847LV00002BB